NATURALLY IT IS NOT.

A POEM IN FOUR LETTERS

callie gardner

contents

(proem: against nature)

'nature' was invented to separate wholes from their parts,
things from each other, and us from the rest of the world.

so:

this poem(s) is against nature:
against the cycle
of birth,
growth,
decline,
death,
& renewal
against the compulsive reproduction of that, & also this
pernicious idea that "growth" is good,
which started off as just a preference for one
time of year over another but now
thanks to the false equivalency of nature & culture
is destroying the world.

i wrote the springletter in cardiff,
in the midst of the end of study and its economics,

i came up with the summerletter in california,
the land of eternal summer and perpetual drought,
& on the hebrides, my summerisles,

& then i wrote the autumnletter in glasgow
where i was born, grew up, & am from
but where i was only then living for the first time as an adult
which is sort of fitting or nicely non-fitting
because its motto is let glasgow flourish which is to say

let glasgow put out flowers, pollinate, & grow
(which it did, as the second city of the empire,
disastrously) but the symbol of the city
    celebrates its infertility –

                the tree that never grew.

    finally i wrote the winterletter in leeds
      on a very short temporary contract,
          in a damp flat,
      teaching highly canonical and often shit drama,
      my panning those plays for liberatory potential
      inflecting the poem.

    i found as i worked and revised i was confirming some of the ideas
about the seasons
    i was hoping to destroy.

the springletter had a spirit of creativity,
    the summerletter was joyful,
        the autumnletter contemplative
            and the winterletter often miserable.

i don't really know what to say about this
except that i think my own experience of the art and culture of seasons
has coloured my own reading-back of this work
    and that i hope anyone else who reads it
    will be able to find the wintriness of the summerletter
    and the contemplations of spring,
      and that it's lucky, and
finds readers who are contrary enough
    to make it do something for all seasons.

springletter

Who has not been sleeping on an inspired day? The
mind of the day sleeps us. Watching us. A fascinated
consciousness.

(carla harryman)

in the fringes over and above where reading
touches, some spring begins. by this i mean:
some elevated selection, with water or blood absorbing
perpetual wisdom, dominates and defines the bright downdraft
in the teeth of or against the serious
snow.

      under it, grass blued out of spectrum
(its designs laid over 'innocent' photomemory) unbreathes its
rattle into the corrie-cup of declining winter: at
last, here it wanders up the mountain path,
having wound a thread a thousand miles around
this much land.

          in grief, terrain touches some
new feelings. paradisiacal storms have done a similar
knitting, glamour-bombed what space has yet been voided
by intent to purchase yet or buy to
let. a land tax in the asteroid belt,
a minimum gravely bent adoration following new travels

by windlass. witness: 2822 sacajawea deprived of being

uprisen, unbuilt domain of which we become part.

pacific pallor, grey interior: different fightings of wars

combine into unregistered teenaged telegraph of a myth,

a parodic reversal: see countless grassroots ann claybournes

of the solar smash the system sabotage growth

gratia growth. physics needs a little help from

the friends of the anything but the earth;

since this self-replicating pattern escaped the gravity well,

one treacherous exo-terrorist cell tables a perpetual motion

to abandon the foisted project.

                              on this planet,

there are some soft guarantees when we consider

wishes and nature, the primary colours of debate

exclusionary in print, additive in the light show

and, in petrichoric pigmentation, sensitive to things' being

as dust. *And it is well to state*

that rain makes hills green / And the sky   Stein, *Stanzas in*

blue and the clouds dark / And the water   *Meditation* (II:iii)

water by them, but as we own, idiom

lands on both sides, encoding empire.

                              blast windows

protect an insect colony comprising so many species

that there is no longer species, only individuals

and nuance. the children who come to beg
at the butterfly box decry this unrealistic practice:
biodiversity of (say) a tree gives no cue
for laddering the way up, shredding the bark
for functional biologies to proliferate in layers. nothing
less than lesson is crayoned approval: losing legs
makes the colony collapse to standing in the
face of criticism. *What is a utopia for?*

Barthes,
Roland Barthes

To make meaning. at the first interrational congress,
a paper of losing: manifesto of the *irréalisable*
(which is not to speak of lost in
lotus, but of easy pose marshalled with all
amicable might). the fruits of frequent subtheorising hold
every body is a utopia: unmobilisable force meets
an unmakeable object, and the deep resulting pore
of atopia is here to rain stopped play.
tangled together in their streets and sheets, delegates
pick significance out of each other's body hair,
reflecting on what's given: the presentation of yelling,
self-effacement in the facing basement of interpersonal noise;
a way to be together adapted into autonomies
proliferating under the sign of (attemptable, achievable) zone;

Raha,
~~countersonnets~~

and *erotogenics intelligible* if only because the alternative grinds us into cricket flour.

                           vegans are hypocrites

if they don't love beetles? how about honey?

or octopus ink? in a world where black

writing can only be sustained by notation donation,

secular joy comes from *disjecta membra* eightfold censorship.

what to say though to that collapsed cellular

factory when it brings joy. (what to say

to mars, boating on the hellas basin.) blue-deep,

are there other shades in the black?

                               hold

in abeyance, this flotation notation abandons

its claims to disciplined skill, deferring *as syllable*

from sound. peyote wheels down, freely shipping across

a network of gigantic rays, no adequate figure

for mastery; describe that smooth function of alteration

pegged to adoration, or worship, lifting the critical

which alters in turn in new dimensions, delayed

by new-emerging grades. if there would no longer

be anything but differences, in that final term

of fragmentation, where does persistence of desire go?

the question posed as if scarcity is hard

to come by; for while mass action's shelf-life

commodifies into style, and domination needs facing down

Dickinson,
Poem 126

a fair fight, scale unthumbed kinkily nightly; not
that to be differentiated would no longer mean
to be excluded, but that pugnacious, membranous limen
would be motile around dictionary chapters, land, sea
and air.

     driving pegs into each squiggling cartouche
has seemed to be the endgame. or else
a tracker on each, or understanding their cowpaths.
it has often been expeditious to mutilate bodies
in this way, and renegotiation electrified the rails
accountship had seemed to be the day of
order; as it is, *term has an end.*

                                    Forrest-Thomson,
It was getting dark on the platform of   'Cordelia'
nowhere and the cruel stations blatter the windows,
and unenhanced concrete seems to make important points.
rand and/or flies and/or shit prezi the glass
with innovation. we have sat and watched commentators
on this scale and subject with this purpose
like veronica forrest-thomson, the memorable poet, who claims
that term has an end, that there is
a limit.

     limit cases were carved into monolithic game-pieces,
and a private-language argument occasioned by the opening
of a new bookshop. meanwhile on planet earth,

none of this is metaphor, and then deposition
scrawls over the window dirt with sudden asemicv
erve. *Your hands / shake. You are fragile to*[o,]
the world's / noise. You imagine all the others /
sleep on little trains or beetle the lands worth
quicker; finger drums as digital scribble as scream.
what is it made of, aspect?

        so you

would hope, and then with that particle, conceptualising
feminising, subliming to mist. they say that mushrooms have
no seeds, and their stomachs are the world.
this is not meant in the manner symbolic,
astrologic, sentimental. first pioneers tea-garden on a star,
disappointingly cold, cellular origins demanding return. stable
harvest jiving empirically toward a dirt road ascesis,
walker across water which is empanelled under (or
because of) unique movements in and under land.
we furious seldom attend windmills; hail three blithe
birds that never wert at sin down. *I*
do not want to go into that cold
reality, stark as a dream dun mor vaul
protects. those two bays, harvested like front teeth
marks in the yellow diamond of the island. how
its magic panels, covers its hair, modestly un-scathing

Cooke,
'No One Sleeps'

Gunnars, *The*
Substance of
Forgetting

its geodesic scarf; trees live only precariously, present
no peril to the monkey-puzzle.

                                       attendant loss becomes
the velvet failure of each photograph, black goes
green, highlights fade in certain jubilation of kingfishers
predating low over meres demand to be still,
and never not embarrassingly open to variant real.
plato's lecture on the forms was too good
to write down, otherwise starred persistence laid altar-bare,
and as we know, beneficent scribbles become suck,
taken as freely as given and later lost.
(how) ever can't they not be what's said
written on the soul of the hearer together
with understanding, that knows how to defend itself,   Plato, *Phaedrus*
and can distinguish between those it should address
and those in whose presence it should be
silent in the course of things?

                            new apology
                                              ibid.
for old matter: *take a pen and write*
in water, brain-wide, liquid in the face of
quanta that matter. keep solid the free riddance
bidden to gracious growth styled after proliferating vines.
'all' lives rate experience of change by extension
their scale extending changes into reason – livably, transversally –

leaps of clockwork thinking re-leaf and sprout, giving
up into the troposphere the bare of edge.
gradients and built-in angles – of momentum, or series
of sunny shells around – are forms of growth.
it symbolises attractions, but gives no want up.

catalogued over bullshit reams, praxis makes nothing happen
to the seeds in snow. it is recognition
in patterns' time that ensure that category of
things we think of as inanimate, things unendowed
with the capacity to twitch and jiggle remain
snowbound until the thaw; space over air, but
under asphalt is asphalt. what did you bring
out when you thought this was a still
image, what withhold?

Nelson, The
Argonauts

>   *worthwhile pleasures on this earth*
> *slip between gratifying another and gratifying oneself. Some*
> *would call that an ethics*; i however feel
> this new erotics insinuating itself into the space
> left by the turns and contortions of *hermeneusis*:
> apogee extension, lucrative bulk. this holy object depends
> on martial support, hieroglyphic against hieratic in air
> of other minds, and relies on a vector
> to transmit its rimey coordinates, to make discovery

out of ancestral knowledge. without mines, the arcticans
got metal out of meteors – imagine an industrial
revolution founded on a falling sky, summoning ore.
persephonic supposal: we come back from somewhere? we
dialogue, impossibly? keep truth out of the hands
of mastery. personal exploration serves as the avatar
while apology for violence languorises in depths.

                                              against

Arendt,
*The Human
Condition*

wisdom: that which *solves the perplexities of action
as though they were solvable problems of cognition*
signifies in a crop-field spiral. agency of apology
is what can be grammatically said. does this
stay domestic? tinker in the home, we find
bland suppositions in speech proliferate, meaningless as herbs
on the sill. wittgenstein as lover: it is
difficult to kiss anything that is as good
as not kissing anything. if a lion could
fuck, we could not understand when he came.
ludwig asked his students to eat him in
a peach; parameters are frequently retained despite discovery,
so so sorry, kiss kiss.
                      kiss this whittling
naturalistic attraction on a dock. thoreau: walden pond,
what are you doing in here or out there,

in the body farm or incubator cultivating desires.
yoghurt collection, keen pads of some blue fur
what do we need or want from poetic
grist? it is placed one on the other
like growing blank bliss. chase the wolf, taste
tender the peace; unlike making weak, it comes
to be a passion against being predetermined, against
something empirical that is said about bliss; this
is where we need a constructed language of
art-use – pantheon at the minefield where a mythical
response is recorded exploded, a juggling green giving,
until a nice apology peaks over the dividing
wall. i always needed a wreath, but have
marked myself in another way. scraping sponge on
attitude. grasp here: the presence of pine,
sweeping blood-spots into skin and sky.

that soft

talent of positioning is what needs to beard,
fungal against deep patterns, a queer crust and
trust. nothing said in haibun can be repeated
in the court of relation. there we must name
everything that is not nailed down. hypnogogic failure
to return and fasten the font-bath up against
the undersea wall. then, we are in trashy

glow at heaps, corners of vision, leap gaze
fully to the weepy world's off-whirl against gloss
mortal blanched gleaning until a good horror comes,
appling to excess, under the glaze of unexamination.
perceptive coroner grants the state emergence up to
certain limitations and witnesses. make it holy: i
think in swim.

                    a tiny shattered bay waves
from the other side of the sea loch.
in this, find valve, cuticle, shark, and arms,
and turn inwards upon yourself, a pattern scribed
calm and gross on the grounds of dens.
anthropocentric ion, exciting itself in hanging strips. fine force
attracts acts, and mnemonic play crops core heimlich.
nature is only as abundant as it is,
determining history's plundering timescale.

                              selective tor where looking
turns into deed. kingly mount needs an abandoning
rigorous and soft against the appellate torsion wrench
momentum studies in as a factor of factors
and there is a larger question of movement
against the sky – do we need seatbelt, parachutes,
spiky rocks making me uncomfortable in the river?
negative nothing on the cartesian plot. mind, body

split: new ease at eleven, one worry and
ten hopes. healthful drafts populating the sacred, mining
the split; pop-culture pagans gathering in their hedges
after it all dissolves.

                    a general patterncry gets
eroticised in the flesh of anxious energy, which
works as it should: competing ethics offer none
of whatever a person loves. retains selfish will;
adventurous coin despises (but deepens) on tremendous works.
do they need rescued will? i am protecting
a solid glaze. where the transhistorical sex glut
has something to say i will listen; otherwise
the power of sating, reserved for queer protoplasm,
relies on its regulation, a suite of rules
that are coming out to parse significant waves.
it's a truth-routine they mar silken tofu and
plastic marble with (not to bracket a feel,
but vegetarianism is still mass production of proteins,
indefinite chains life-chains, me included) druthers how
something squeaks into motion *swaying is the only*   De'Ath
kind of affection and it comes back to
promised dates which are a mean means to
palliative ends.

               it gets active at the inlet

(choke point or bottleneck would be too evocative)
and dreamers work in the multifarious paisley of
night skies, retaining walls against light drying up
as they level light handwrits in an addicted
pattern. bus unlively for sun or an ancient
chinese encyclopaedia that, from a distance, looks like
flies. categoric hypnosis likes to see artists work
for pay, pigeons in the yard or fellows'
garden.

       apoplectic verve, optional will, formula for success;
all join the panel at conference boom. sounds,
like ears, are two at a time, drained
unlit out of the impermanent slough, sub rosa
for something more deepgreen inked. need a main
original olive to stain the whole action, tiny
giant hands of the mole. trust it to
pattern-alternate that squeak, it's the mass production (me
included) protean, procrustean debs stacked each high against
an emotional wall. well worth living, the nice
guarantee.

       what wakes the plan? ah peace, iron
made more sense than wine for the sea.
what are the responsibilities of metaphor? nothing like
nothing, like nothing there is. i meted out

merry, a will in the face of scrapes
that, bloody, well up at the other signed
of hearings attendance, the wedding of the
century to the decade. fat terrain of wordiness
will get carved into a landscape halt, the
most remote.

     list of things this class all
know: cooking-oil smoke points, beeching axe closures, places
to eat in european cities (not capitals), despairing
about money they give something away. chip up
to the advanced shoulder, genetic genesis of a
fine idea. *offering up in sacrifice a little
of my imaginary*, dreaming up examples of meticulously
accurate yes, securely installed. code is the air,
which is this maintenance of a hard-won fear, flightless
like a mere bird. icing green, allowances escape
something awful into the old cold. can't make
too many selfish adjustments, calculating space, triangles against
power. we hold return to be the most
fashionable of angles of approach. and trends in
consciousness make you one of the bad guys.
back to meat: horse-hoof, warp, whorl, or woof,
it is a loud spontaneous noise, a traffic-jam
in that snared brain city of those metaphoric

Bensmaïa,
*The Barthes
Effect*

18

pains. always sailing they'll come, but never do.

two things: first, what seems like nature is
always already becoming additive and going beach-white with,
bleaching rot. a warm slimy colour-word invades vocabs:
revolutionary modernist will heaps added icons, sage blame,
onto the teeth of questioning, macabre as fellows.
second, there are next to no repositories draining
public time that allow an alternative account of
daffy-secular camp diaristics; what it means to bleed
from your genitals in a therapy session doesn't
need the psychopathology of everyday life to sort
it out; nevertheless, a range of industries has
been sprung from that sticking-place but nobody seems
willing to be clearly headfabrickedly into the swirling
perturbation of marriage, artily debit abjection to peacable
fucking in the void of synonymous hollow hoping
roll of dream (a requisition, a need).
                              draw
the best possible environment. i'd like to find
out about your work from gothic paralleled idiom,
but i hope at least we will lavish
views on the waiting year. unconscious drama playing
out lying on the cheesegrater, deformation of script

the arms and legs make notable as drained
sour stomach acid remnants. eat repeatedly that which
it has not needed when it creates audible
hope, will wishing across deep water table applying
to more situations.
                    add it to hell. deny
transformations will swipe at the belly of this
one ship-in-the-night golly gotham piecemeal approach to two
paired ways of being. that alteration *being compelled*
by our own opacity, our own places of
unknowingness in the face of the face. see
the slaver of painted labour, see the weeks
establish themselves painted on drain. horrorcross paints on
erroneous (that i love to be) sloping futures
animate erratic spores.

Butler, *Giving
an Account of
Oneself*

                    accede to rest-breath apology. maintain
spiralling hopes. that short word has privileged access
to brainpan basics, has a new impression left
on a nightly chest. the mole medical advice
tells us is city-sized – cathedral, university, public transport
system in dire need of investment – lives weakly
in that way. jots populate the sky above
a line of dermal scribing, reductive to say
this reduces: what do you mean all. harsh

buzz mellows the ears, puts in gold appearances
on silver-oxided stages. weather system chew-toy festival season
alters patterns for the decade and its marriage
to the century. cry doom and split with
the thunder-denying hoard of things; sets made out
of these hold badly to theory, which in
turn makes weird terrors invade childhood-robbed sleep.

                                                          lines

weaved out of this fabric warp it unchangeably,
keeping fingers bloody, (making) ankles muddy as they
splinter and sink in the sand. where are
precious perspex sandy breaks again, not breathing for
fear they will be paid and involved in
cravings dreams against armies of anything, mobilised in
the general defence of the specific against ongoing
self-identification? with will and whisk and partitive mail
where glass resists coming upon blood in long
series of tests. termination remains a placeholder; worms dance
in sample sizes too small.

                    green above all,

the marmoreal veiny worth protects passion whose rote
rot makes meaning in a series of suitable
shades. graves yawp with the effectiveness of false
permanence, granted while all subliminal and smaller fades

and moulds bloom in the corner, more cities
getting bigger and lives in them little to
make out of what is left, cornering paint
and establishing corners out of a lot we
make and work on and do.
                        broad segmentation:
the irritant arc of hap returns everybody's eyes
aren't a dark liquid, instead are filament corrosive
to partipatterned domes of rough wind. daring partly
ambitious to be aimed, making heartburn meritocratic on
the lake, drained-out apocryph of watery hieratics. arrow
indica in the valley, where cultures of writing
grow like mould, beard and bloom. the real
rhomboid polity in great graves are in making,
and amazing, soldiers in the dream spat out
sorrel which has cleaned the traps, basing a
bat flying against wake is a green apology,
meanly supposing of course that i can effluviate
reflective resident but can't peace, won't authorise work,
make it rain in the playa. flat priestly
tones ingratiate fantasm watching it walk out, sicklily;
indeed, never imagine a hot number needs play,
instead, sheaves clapping annotate breeze.
                                this is that

farm-considered natural apology twisted epiphyte read as vocalic
glyph. i am my obsession with graphemic mania,
reaming motile inks out over each well. cliff
loaded, castle burnt. with my septum pierced i
finally will be a good subject of discourses,
in the end will let loose a fire
and nose-noise flood.

               how does fit, cold wind
demand we dress? it's like a centralising force
is a black swallow, given everything and put
back on the shelf among engraving, for now
satis, although if i'd known choral rupture would
have malformed error i'd have done. kneading straight
sorrow i work for no money and hoard
my days. filth is bourgeois clean ill mess
of ness.

      at that landhead, reassess. give over
wild im and ex to the draping animations,
lord-leightonly cloth of that which deep down needs
press. the place which is not one says
too much to be translated: i need grey
home, the product of a post-ethical recess.

                   plantfight
moaning over what's not real, the captured flag

to the draining thrill of rule. to spin
fast fascinators, kidding and granting *the park*
where state translators, laid off, sat sad for
their hospitals, prisons and schools infinite amounts of
land. (in this, ambitious progeny retreat
and are slick on the soles of feet
that make a living out of wandering, birds
in the partial lights screaming interpreted as jazz.
real paid mentions in populations' feeds and bought
followers, adaptations of the marked egg to consequences
and the private lives of self-replicating systems. ideas
of the present run on incompletings, get rid
of impermanent mutations to make outside modes irrelevant
to inquiry. tourist board gives off a savage
bleat. it has reduced the century married to
the decade married to the millennium to the
ash-pile fervently examined in nonstandard panic about history
which then doesn't become something else. archaeologic heaves
unplugging conches variefacèd from ancient economies to floridian
finance, a mangrove miracle in widely imagined deeps
while mountainheights demurely defer. it's missing, that eurotic
blandishment, giving over a keenly green-blue ink musk
sybaritic-symbolic, like crownless elms, and the repeating pattern

in their leaves.) pink slime grants an apology
over the west-wreaking will.

                                   united in faith apeing
bullshit arguments it is academicon (monkey c., monkey
due) in the rust when we are rhetors
only to bleed blips. compilation video is learned
behaviour, needing scrip to export. alternative comings look
like other wheels, yet they are spoked for,
and civics hubs the main, riddled with astroverge;
norms are denied approvals. but here's some shit
to return to loam with:

                     if *the joy*
of life is the irresistible, constant, victory of
the new, then there is no return; if
sadness, like apology, lurks at the eye of
bliss, then getting ruptured out of your situation
is as lunular as it is lunar (the
fuck it's cyclic); and if colophonic irrigation persists
past bonds set up to let us fail
(which is, since this is time for plaindealing,
to say, if books need both our fear
and disobedience to go on), then scrippling is
as perceptive as the copyright declaration on manifestoes
that transformed mimeographed life. don't read pedagogical critique
of flight school when you are up in

Kandinsky,
'On the
Problem of
Form'

the air; official advice says shut your eyes
during plane crash scenes. if when you pay
you tick that box that says yeah, offset
this with a tree, what does it look
like inside. rings of hot pink and sap
of gold, leaves hang like big sloppy blossoms
in the maladaptive conditions surrounding weather. consider this
a letter, sheaf sigil matched with sea, see?

summerletter

Like love, the slowest and most statistically unreliable of human communications mediums, reading is a failed lesson in bureaucracy and poetry its most indolent operation.

(tan lin)

a new plan disrupted is sheer hierarchy
yet its form relies on falling at first hurdles

i have come to feel sharpened on the edge of this apology
a range of acceptable responses self-presents its health
a panel constructed in white

under review this street beckons
at and against its augury

error perhaps is the nicest way
of coming to know something

it's better anyway than a series of reptilian biases
ghosts in the paradigm
(as nostalgic as its and our computational selves)
who acknowledge that the only way to win
is to give the sign up to play

suffice to say it should never have happened
the wrong words in the wrong way assembled
which is to be as wicked as we are sorry
a manner which is to be regarded as unreserved grief
and modification to have flesh is to be embarrassed by it

since having belongs to the same frame
the same graphic network of signals and responses

deep sorrow –
retrieve this retraction
accountable anger for what should never have been said

hold your temper loosely or like a fish
it will flop out of your hand and away
babbling upstream like an echo, fragment,
utterance:

eyes resetalking boo beashing againly,
l in arly municise ske to bookset
and a metalletterust ter
ing; hottom the ight reset
and in ponotlin isense
talk an arly mes thold, hold, talke to
cominn ofall ight row
a for part-scend be punicipulledesceng;
ho matinhabith languag wise thing boore
thabited to o beat so abited to body

we h
langainsthe wof
bodand in a ring g booke to the beforear eng; how's to mat
cops to ating to a masses
wildion
munic
marke to gushinter massed that insiget lith
lanyoned to inter, insike to beasense
the lighthing with
befonds w

this is open season on psephologic failures
winding down spirals for being too sad
for looking up and watching danger flash
in points of the eye

skidding against slime
i was watched by some hateful high look
in a paranoid suspension of ball-bearings against radar

going through time in this way i wish you were here
someone to be addressed with an art (of) apology

great is the artifice of the ephesians
sublimated into a pound-prayer to diana
a train-prayer to mercury
a festival-prayer to thoth

my scribbled map contains islets and rivers
peace(able) ou(s)t

but summer in the city is the only summer
having been rusticated to smaller cities & towns by study
and habit
and economy

summer in the country
(which is made)
is a commodity
so summer in the city is all that's left

though day trips may be mounted
hiking or ferry rides to an island
ultimately these do not have any of the qualities of life

perpetuated densely under the white sky
city of frank gladness built by hands
which so shielded in the nervous system
oceanic brain
and made strange and metropolised
(change of state)
to the new constructed form

scripting, cleave between horrors
discover subcultures in ice that go deeper than leather
become beloved by people in the know

common-mental balayage
psychic shifts in the mutual vertex of strands

missing leaves between covers have been unstuck
to give ideas more false than ever

a wish is out on a ledge in this way of organising policy –
perceiving motivates pathology like poirot

within sheaves, conceal oddities, & other
genetics will multiply across the planetary domain
the overlap of well-studied
structures of mischance

nobody notices their expression
there's no translation like there is with that
beauty-greedy combination of faces

it accepts all / marks & none.
(myles, 'culture')
what is not cultivated?
barthes, 'pax culturalis' says
(surprise)
it's nothing
because of the green slimy fingers of bourgeois love

these leave distinct traces in the white air
in the speechifying dirt that hangs between people
an illimit of shimmers curtained by neopagan
astrology of the market

can't i not ask
what planet are you from?
perhaps we can fix that
find somewhere nice in the zeta reticuli system
areciboic insistence after a few decades –
wide public support for extending
manifesto'd destiny into space

that's where the marks belong
just write / into it

years ago there eclipsed a climate catastrophe
a moth – and why not?
after all it doesn't prevent a nightly attempt
to read our own expression
full of bland unwisdom
and those small sillinesses
suffer what they must

but as their detector
their ray clock
travels through darker valleys
flat u-shapes carved by glaciers
alaskan sliders lubricious with lack of will
that nasty butterfly returns
its emigrant wings paper sleeves for ransomed
analphabetic unwritingness
itself a fiction in the shadow of occulting star-clouds
oppositional coronas
so would it be better to say
crowns of no value
(itself an inheritance)

the eyes of the road seem fixed

making a study of blueness while travelling
we had some tremendous luck

here i will give some examples of things that are blue

infinite library stretching off in all directions
just begging to be jumped out of
that's what this tiny thing is like on the motorway

in a small country everything is so close
and the view from inchmurrin is not that from big sur
get your bum off of my dharma

this is the problem of how to howl
it has another name in every language
ow, aïe, oy, ach, itta

it all comes in a flash
each erasing the last
there's none so twinkly as them who will not breathe

they bend themselves to the door
a windy night of technocratic feudalism under the stars

dotlike existence
(unmarked)
promised by that progression in a pinwheel
around the northern eye

angelic galleries dehisc in stages
the world-beetle divinely constructed
puff on it to get it to make that final hop
out of the window of a moving summercar

this is the source of what makes the light
that releases the flash, that replaces the last
an erasure unbuilding a gain

they do not like to be pulled only,
lack an apart-sense, with language the inn of body

lettering gushing against wise skin
is that which
applied to beastly causes
will feel metallic
marketing books to a squat

we hold, talking, to mating shells
trust those names that fall in a row
a theme and a mess get light reset
and inter in ponds what copses nearly massed against:
municipal trouble

condescend to an uninhabited adverse nation
before the bottom seems to anyone's eyes to be
coming; how's this for insight: near enough for pain,
the thing is the world

my nine favourite substances come in recipes
(nothing is natural, nothing is free)
this one is made of
vegetable oil, castor oil, citric acid, and mica

the pale eyes of a deep-sea creature
suddenly look mine out of the face into a mirror

released into the world by tutenkhamun
like a benign curse

it turns faces into unfamiliar bodies before us
by its absence
i have always found my own strangeness
my materiality comforting
the natural body
being a product of those naturalist's sketches
the voynichian diagrams
is a trap-code
but the kohl pencil is in my hand

how long does it take to starve
under different forms of government?
will this one let you?
or are you hectored into living?
health the lossless state that makes possible fear
beauty the loss-leading rational vector in a seller's market

counter this with the bewitching power of bodily fats
to layer through a past self-concept
living like the replicating scales of one's own dragon
body-horror blooming in the cleft between
a total randomness of shapes
that eject reproducibility
projected between screens
doubled shades proving wave-particle clusters
of imperfect metaphor
layered thickly on the body of knowledge

they are with body, that which they will market

toes in a set of early liquid terms
trouble habitation through nothing like lack
languishing at applied feelings, holding narrowness
internally against strong being
you are coming to sight
pain is not of the letterwise

to write a book, automate names
a gate to what've opposed consistent in any cradle
the world pulled apart in white skin
because of squeaking shells
or the light of corporate funding demands bottom manner

the eyes' only sense of body is as metal
but it is trusting and responds to the communal universe
before eyes

what kind of clarity
and what kind of water?
fern-feather, encoding chromosomes for a million years
crabs gather and are taken apart
by a sign for the south pole
penguins 16,200 miles

it was hoaching yesterday
grim weeks seen in all weathers makes it easier to leave

a few more days of silence

what would it be like if this were two islands –
uninhabited, a pair of soays?
abandoned monastic cells visited by tiny ferries?
causeway-joined giants' feet?
what is the centre of that gyro-geo
scoping-graphing
process by which we establish our relationship to the world

graphic bliss: before painting, music (barthes)

some of them can feel with the *swerve* of a phrase line
and key signatures set off a drama
in the red acidic soil of the mindpan landscape

hierarchy of the arts:
music always knows best,
the misty mountain
to the lush, low plains of painting
or the deep gardening that writing is

here, however, is that hike of geologic knowledge
where the symbology reveals the structure to view –
crystalline, stacked, alien
but recognisably, translatably, an art

walking on something's back in this way
is the most alienating way of coming to know it

whether it's linguistics or physics
something is replaced in domination
by the clock and punchcard
a discipline and punish
brazil machine scrollwork
chirography of no apology

and, as if to model is slotted mineral
the workings of universes
the floor of rooftops arcs grace-bidden out of godways

light-fingered across the keyboards –
dvorak, maltron, turkish f –
or with respect to the touch of pens
stealing parts of language that remain missing (yau)
you are shoplifting from a language that belongs to
this priest before it belongs to you

and yet tundishwise it all trickles
back down into spontaneous utterance

demanding frankness, we programmed a computer
to throw yarrow
to trade futures or allocate resources thereby
strangely, the market by oracle flourished
and grew at unprecedented rates

movement and the rest have their definite laws;
according to these,
firm and yielding lines are differentiated (i ching)
they cross, approach at angles, reassess,
such that the law is apologised for and corrected
maybe autonomously

of course, there were flaws
excesses, human errors of interpretation
however, it was still better
than the economy of lucid dreaming
mere intuition
or the tarotic systems of our enemies
massing their forces behind the velvet curtain

jesuit language science would have us understand that
despite that great favour done to us by
the squishy mouths of the ancient greeks
in chinese, *a well-turned sentence*
is as much stripped of all intermediaries
as is the most rigorously bare algebraic demonstration
(fr. amiot) –

utopia-of-writing, i met you in a dream
wherever fine books are cold to the
mental/astral feeler touch

but it falls to the realist to acknowledge that
in verse, a well-tuned sentiment
is as majorly fucked in all contexts,
as is the least real bare life we lead as literary symbols

sleeplessness: external brain

i have to write down my thoughts for them to make sense
because by the time i get to the end of a sentence
in my mind the beginning has died

the incoherency of speech is a loss-leader
in the anagrammatic economy of thought and wakefulness

going through time in this way prompts the art of apology
forslept pressures suggest messy wire loci
sizes increased and flattered to provide clarity
make them into ideogrammatic particles
abandoned drift chance (cf. macdonald,
'after the war')

they are gathered together
who left by this form and circular reason eater

no public / no republic
so much founded on the living room, coffee shop,
& museum

nothing to spend money on is the same as no money at all

vital in the slough
i want to look at the white sands and ogham
(this is where it's written, a qelticism)

where are the faeries-ferries and ethereal foxgloves
catching in the wind?
a snail with a car as its shell
here a slug on the path
here a vole
here a rabbit on the white sand
here a dog following bikes on the road
or a croaking bird on the rough isle

no justice no peace
while gilt and silver stand for nothing being regulated
and waves, voices, erroneous dust
cotton, silk, and ermine perfected
mine the tours

when the old dream of revolution shatters
into little ones of wealth (bad old story)
the domed horror is gold
indeed i think nothing is the same
that salvages two conventions twice

keep heavy metals coming out of the clouds
it's a baneful ideation on wry, bred
(or sprouted)
in the house of nuance, calendar dump
back up or down load

make it a mutinous sign or bound
everything that comes out between arches

this lochan is reed city
where are you rushing off to?
greed-furred geological fingers feeling blind
generative insights populating maps

england is now a dark green tunnel
of worry; is ever far-northernness a shield or shadowy
disguising cloak?
on this alien island so near its birth
every landscape collected in the magic-hour sun-rain
serendipitous beauty of birches –
the reeds grow like beards, like armpits,
like woven wet chests, like forgotten patches

these live and scatter themselves
against the cartographic crimelook
of the scrip na-multiplies, h-everything,
invisidhible consonthanants making the language thick,
ancient, and safe

consider, who read old texts on virtuous things:
what's the bright beauty
its stone chokehold on oceanic living?
lifted from somewhere else –
heavily laden across the internet, legislated
scrip kiddie is told –
severed wildly against bankrupt billions
left sublimating from the time, guiltily

at internally rotating times,
these are the virtues offered

(the gods love it because it is typically done by beautiful people)

natural changes are irreversible and entropy
is not (only) a fascist repiling of embers
in the policy shops of the weft

now she wonders if the laws of seasonal renewal
might apply to humans too (kraus)

soon it turns, the reek in the social lum
and i become goma basement
coma patient, hiding from revolution
-ary possibilities in a progressive institution

& the highest levels of status quo government
fight over rewrites to busted fantasies and cover-ups

'public confidence has only grown'
& we're left with all we're allowed to have known,
because now there is a wise
reprise of that argument that gives you
that look in those dried-out eyes
a record number of parks and gardens open 24 hours
so you can come after work
as long as you don't bring your own flowers

dream the abstract
something social:
beauty not coming
at the seams seems ineffable
colour-trumpets heraldically flush
but so tidy a system is bound to be whisked away

hard science wrecks a will
stands in for demolition
girlish on the face of it
and even improved has us running scared
phlogistonic itch for something part of that impenetrable
membranous medium between sense and nature

(neither of course being material
matter'd be better
and more separable and isomorphic
and thicker/muddier/wetter
and effabler
which (however) would be a change
nothing else counting but unnatural
inseparable (ah) matter (made of light))

the list of ways they use to make matter real

surely maintenance is conservatism
or is that the etymological fallacy at neverwork?
rough cities are dreamt of in the face of falling stock

how are long times preserved
how are stocks and bones
how are faces and shins
how are futures and shorts
or gold winters made up?
there's nothing concrete
and it comes out of how we treat that sound, our son

the low temperatures at which biles
and other humourous flavours boil

stains living in woods are trees
cat-patterned, tortoise-shelled,
rabbit-tailed, barnacle-bottomed, sea-scraped

what matters is shaped by the directions taken
that allow things to appear in a certain way (ahmed)

if it matters, it is because of the movement it makes
through space (and) in relation to other things
and if something *does not matter* it is because
its movement blocks appearances
engendering that abnegative death
the death by blockage

blocked lives claim their mattering by eruptive means
mapped across and with history

whatever happens in the guts happens
at the product of convergent lines

overlapping patterns here of bodily winds –
not only (your) sirocco smell
but your velocity, heat, and consequences

(of course
i should not be attempting this project
which could have to add to the grand storehouse of writing
the 'numberous wordhoard' to which my idle idols contributed
their development as souls and scholars
and i will soon let you discharge your readerly responsibility
or obligation and come to the end of this text

afterwards there will be no need for art
because every experience will be performance
every room an installation
every utterance and notation a poem

islands of paper against the rising time

the following & foregoing add nothing,
mean nothing, see and act on nothing at all.)

indo-european *debacle of the neuter:*
massive shift [...] to the masculine form
and feminine = derivative (barthes)

our eyes reset
taking repetitively that beast
that lurks and is over and over again
communal, municipal
government by the ghosts who inhabit type

most of the local population was employed
in the printworks
i sense an early linguistic mess tholed
holed up and talked to
coming in for a language or fall

under the influence of wild ink
the waterfall seems to reverse itself
when i wake up and inhabit language
i bear a wise thing and abut it with my hol'd body

either we know
(gathering intelligence from all sources)
or we don't know
(whispering in the flowerbeds or the alleys)

or either we know
(rooting around in the landfill)
or we don't know
(mooning over a piece of info)
or we neither know nor don't know
(that was later found in the recycling)

or either we know
(how many formal logic symbols
can i tattoo on my lower back)
or we don't know
(this now is a full alphabet)
or we neither know nor don't know
(room for one more)
nor neither know nor don't know
(syntax error a beautiful animal)

call me email – *shipmates*
have ye shipped in that ship? (melville)
composed new and saved and been bounced to spam

history is the engagement with all forms of life
the tree-octopus or drop-bear
they come in forested agglomerations
all our doings were biomass
but we were going to moth our way out

instead it is meatcanned
this containerised version of us gives up its bones
weakens its millennial grip on the next age

we were larval once
but without exchanging a cell
somewhere in this circumnavigation we became
in the creaking ancient timbers of shipped steel
just worms

giving a book or writing a lecture about your failing health
your knees or stomach trouble or skin complaint

you are coming to compline in a rough garment
and holding forth later in a nightgown

even though feelings of pain
have the demands of abstraction applied to them
they are internally consistent as a set of corporate byelaws
and nothing like a rothko in the manner
in which they will relate to the market

pain is only popular because of early support and funding
from the cia, which opposed it to the notion
popular under full communism
of *no* pain

independent agglomerations of independences
a treaty with seven billion signatories

no surer way to date a piece of writing than to line it
with the light of irrelevant stars

a territory ascribed to unchecked markets
another to unchecked cooperation

when i put my feet through heather
i lose my sense of wright and run
when i wriggle my heel in white sand
i can feel myself squeaking
against the seashells in the bathroom
then when i turn my toes in the carpet
i understand nothing natural will be revealed
by the stripping away of culture like paint from a baseboard

bone knitting like cat's cradle
hands entwined against being pulled apart
to only get stronger
coded strong nose
(like how coffee is strong)
and road-warm, hill-brown;
different parts of my body are a small, communal polity

fully automated luxury
languishing at the bottom of holme fen engine ditch
in a moment of abstraction (forrest-thomson)

i am a pig reader
with eyes of pig-iron and pyrite
fake metal for false visions

trusting in the face of seer-satori
sweetly-set up facing the dimming

we visit the last planet in the universe
persisting only in our context

president announces apology tour of the colour-wheel
fifties housewife battle groups assemble to protest
and take down industry

show me your hands

it meant being infected by a religion like any other
a strong white accustoming to budged balloons

stand in the shelter and something comes out crying

blue for the madonna and red for strong martial
men and boys
after the switch, coats still bloody were washed whiter
for the little girl soldiers of pink supremacy

the ideology of girlhood –
honouring tears
rehearsing endless care
– retains after stone-beaten washes

grey opens and yellow admonishes
while pink thinks

without suffering they never went long
sylvia rivera is still alive
kickstartering her heating bill
(though probably not in summer)
and meanwhile revolutionary action
is struck blind andor
used to set-dress a new subplot
in the grand cons piracy

kathy acker starred a rat in her
pussy king of the pirates
and ching shih pirated all oceanic dithering
of the age
turned it turn this wise
spirited back to its origins
the argument from progress
democracy, or human nature

unhope ever
surely an anachronism

definition of progress:
doing the same thing over and over
and expecting a different result

the rough isle, the black lake
the place you drag your boat across
generalise all of these names
towards the little atlas of living

i am imagining densely printed columns and contour lines
and the same handful of words written over and over

isthmuses of tarbets, columns and straits
kyles etched ideogram style, letterwise
on eilann garbh, petroglyphs that predate habitation
that are attested before eyes

dangling your feet off some jumping off rock
off lochann dubh

those always have folk names though
a catching of the water of the language
in what've you got there for narrowness of hands

communal with body, the world responds, pained
to come with insight to its senses in a book with terms like
'skin' & 'fundament', language's bottom mating

what narrowness seems pulled from marketing
before language has had enough has nearly
nothing whatever to do with early language, a liquid

it all responds by drawing near to lack, by coming
to a municipal active fault, with you holding –
having applied the mess-book – to descending
lack, holding enough nearly-skin to end
the strong before-sense which automates trust

the corporeal universe marketing insight:
this coming to the manner is only a feel

keep holding out for the frosty commission:
against that kind shiver, i need a summermind

some corries hold snow all years –
and are here with seeded crevices
disbursing toward scree

with wind blowing in the same bare place
they can find a spirit within themselves
of the eye and location

it's hard for the listener to recover that level
of representing sound by geological echo
and recovery speech

dunes are made in a process of systematic wind
watching hot hills come in from the cold
caught transparently in an iced droplet –
cough, and make it return peaceably time over time

there is a pleasure in the pronoun game
in the steppingaround
(enactment of) taboo

ask and proceed / continue to wonder –
does something make it burst for itself into that social-
setting surface superego glue

satori as solidarity is not going to hold water –
inactivity as a metaphor for peace

that as the active concept, not lack of war
as a bastardised, impenetrable gully becomes
neptune's staircase, nude descending
the inverted forest planet in the water table

there's none so blinky as them who will not sea
but who rather know what the insides of their eyelids
look like in motion

there's none so bored as those who will not tea

sortes sinensis, book of the tasseology
a connoisseur's (dilettante's)
guide (needing guidance)
textbook of texture
manual of random footerings with the spoon

custom is pristine, but connection a horror
thus we train hard from birth to berth in

a sparkling city of hill-industry
must yet have twea quarters where they practice
and sell by the 100g
the art of the useless supplement (barthes)
milk first or after?
sacraments of the aesthetic religion of tea-ism

the way of the tea:
what goes up the hill must come to town

what would it mean to have 'wept'?
i understand crying intellectually
but to be at one with one's own brackish waters
i think would be to have one's own complex of self
be like the lochs that
unmappably, unprovably, unundarstandably
dot the alien landscape here

they are called the islands of the strangers
(excepting the music of their speech, airy erse tones)
and are strange themselves

there is a broch where a lord was once betrayed
on this kind of internal water
the 'island of bad counsel'

is this the counsel
we take from the stones and sparse, unhandplanted trees

what would it mean to have been kept?
this sociopathic bird is following me

we raised the sanity waterline especially for him
but still he hunts, skippingly, in the sound

the figurehead will be returned
when the boat retakes its rightful place in the water
floating machair-light
refracting late-evening sun through all the colours
of the 'corn' this island calls
the deep, old management of its many grains

the ferry arrives and departs
to the inscription of hills
grey-green for black
functioning as crisp-edged block-letters
soaking out of the other side of the papery mist

the fact remains however
that any phobic response to the mutation of song
that rests upon the fiction of taking the line of the mind
on this brisk walk will,
despite how endlessly and freedom-lovingly it insists
on the stability of the heart of its vowels
become *lost in the cleave of clasping and sweetfleshed day*

(whitman)
a bit of him suffices even in this bliss-kept,
white-scarfed, hottening endless summer of the letter
whose brush-stroke is found not in the shape or face
but in the movement of the ink-dark,
link-stark, minch-ark sea

what a favour (says barthes)
the greeks did the world
with their idea to write down the vowel

in any event, it proved a gate to that *fleshy, mucous, liquid
body, the musical body*
that definitively says what and where the world is
and how to be a brain in its vat

yet it's that that responds to light
an abstraction if ever there was

retreat from the crystalline lip
come back to what's real
to reel
tape is something you can touch
be shocked and react to
no world made out of data
is really real
like matter real

any statement of utopian vision
in this void scriptable discipline
more preposterous there is not

babies grown in vats?
fine
fully automated communal production?
i can show you some spreadsheets
hive minds uploaded to the computer?
happens every day

but dare the spinning engines
of the zeppelin, gherkin of the other

doing anything would be to explode publicly
ending the discourse for generations to come

global helium shortage and the moon
means it is space travel too,
but whoopee
if you can write your way to the back of the vacuum
hey i trust you that you can sell anything

ok ok
somehow i thought maybe no but yeah you are right ok

yeah but as you say it's yeah ok
in context i mean i thought this might be
a problem for you
it's not a problem for me
but if it's a problem for you it's not ok

ok then

isn't there anything else you want to ask
before things go ahead no ok

i feel ok

i'm glad things are ok with you now
i don't like going around thinking you are not ok

it's ok by me

and we go around imagining things which are ok

they're through with seems
there where they lurk's got whatever insights on common causes
the will of enough letters
trust pained by coming trouble

shift applied wild my
my being employed
or feel
be that automatic skin in the long game
consistent for a world with nothing at
which responds manners to some sense of wake

ghosts mating early condescend
their sight a trust apart from 'skin' and 'fundament'
despite a vision of a deep old supplement

cause derived from bottom feeling
does not matter like a brisk walk will
up before what was nearly mess
circular holding most narrowness

indexpoem to the summerletter

anarchy, apology,

babble

brexit, city, cleavage, culture, cyanide, dharma, draught,

echo

eyeliner, fat,

fragment

gigha, graphic bliss, hand, i ching, ideogram, insomnia, island,
jubilee, juncaceousness, kalotype, library, luminiferous
aether, materialism, matter, modesty topos,

neuter

null, oceanics, pain, phalanstery, personhood, pink, queer,
scotland,

segment

snow, tact, tea, uist (north), uist (south), voice, vowel, zeppelin,
zero degree,

zwitter

autumnletter

and I have known
despair that the Face has ceased to stare
at me with the Rose of the world
but lies furled

(john wieners)

what else
never
grew?

let glasgow compost: a chance for this black swan or falling star to return to the earth as wormwood wormfood. this is no diss; i want to be here til the last days, getting eaten by the maggots with the best of us. there is warming, patterning, in the shanghai'd commune, ok? flecked forming of which homes the swan-staged thorn forest defence system as a postpropositional tooth / truth. fail no disaster, star sprite from balconette, by eyes, dotted in sanction; next, legion of beats, directed home.

loamish draining of long eyes, critical mill of the edible evening. primate psychology is liquid carbon on the surface, rampant across the bergs like a solar shade, layered & glisted like the moon under serious review. wild eyes,

done with
the chart

wild eyes: gag of a moderate principle dots dinosaur-fluttered semiotic system bus. who has cartilage grown into a speak, & in that time *with our pistil soul-bright / our stamen-heaven* [(celan)]. in whose worlds do we live at the small circle of all magnificent soaps.

s l i c e

my eye with a fruit knife, no surrealist craft project but a red poppy, blue or blonde style image system:
change of state
these abstraction migrants are scratch-tested for allergies that go on to burn holes in our nights' pretence to suicide manoeuvre from the other side, which put cracks in a relic button from the long islanders, erased from the portrait of the imaginary tree, the abandoned project wall. the key sometimes to a mind was break, spaces to some, or a guarded graven motif.

wild, gagged eyes of a moderate principle, master so many things. surrounding the
back in local arms
new people's palace (lost so that their loss is islands – cultural & deemed everyone) up to a national park, becomes secretive, express facts blackened, lax up against / freed to the money survives, revolves around a shorthand issue. lie on, sleepy devils; carved

galactic flag crissing & crossing, lax also in white rooms, their dopplerian song derivative – then they make themselves present to our need. shapes of faces run a small press, a series of scaffolds.

there was a time when silly bees could, unwieldy, maintain a set of formal logs; & in that time i was a silly bee. red poppies, blue, or blonde; miss turnip the grocer's daughter has in herself the green of transformation. aortal wind side dude is cornwall-long, across from selfhood or cluster eyes that go up & took down stars straight people subscribe to. a traditional squid belongs beyond life, casing for flying means & the teaselled nostalgia, a bend of squirrelling away beyond a grey & a blue.

thou'rt bound to serve the time

darken and sputter in the baptismal gloaming. on the universe then, the full code. led & then coming there to a place, into the ball of the gaslamp, the totem we have made; reaction in swirls, draining the floor beyond the chemical. an historical reluctance to move, vulnerable, coupled with a need to care for the body with the air. signal-wing flooring its hairiness

pump out the light

83

bellicose to show you the art of belonging which is now being riddled with a wood disease revealing its colour throughout the ark of history.

a planet and its sinister romantic not-water, attained driving at it: meditate on the theme around the shared i. long, it's in with where it's prosaic. what clusters the wall as it might as well rain, wadded out of this, waves in an idea of a truth which is to night around the stars as scarf-silk is to the light-bulb. it is long, and raggedy ann takes away a series of minds bringing under the many-coloured energy the clothes of the think & replacing them with emerald internal sheels, and those for whom a body is legal waste.

bohemia on mars

being lost: a wee transformation. rearranged over the exerted will, done to see the material of that, the model, the what, the mood pattern is, & grant the up-incension from the first up to spaces. spaces, minds, & nights, the (it's really carbon) is japanned, flowers of breast against blame like a dragonfire. we fall to our as-a-cult wrapped skin, the skins between fingers translating into space & then patterns on the insides

hand the sky in

of eyes that look like impressionist paintings of
murices sucking knees.

                        cool over the tied stand ate &
cough in the cold chapel. under the clothes to where
there are these gaps, fingerprints with, what can i
write. what can i say, gaia took the take tied till
september. it can get a question. place that in that
history, & have some diaristic mind question &
replace the bottom-nature; in eyes i am onsite. deep
in a swimming pool in upshaved, in on on
precedence. i have concealed my eye from
overlapping fragments of arms under that tied in
swing of bulb like the fit in miles once you burn up
again. when clothes no longer human tissue flutter, a
leaf a feather, waste our corona red from a hair. swirl
like an e over, o over the thorn, like a weak autumn
cons the source of desire.

                        and mileage fruits & looms,
& swishes that fires the belonging in systems &
spoon eye as the black dress but in a phylactic ding
needing dreams as emetic slough of survival. we
cannot theory-of-mind this busstop. which aren't
we? perform an endless curve into a bone-enriched

*dig for
living*

arsenous bronze in a long bog. to dominate the dwams or old demons, what has come & is draping over & around is (and its many branched bits are) the circulation.

here at the party we wear golden horns, practice our dancing using other people in the human mirror, & the music goes out by touching fingertips. we fail at some note with every brush, a symphony of & noises. this art work performed without the aid of microphones or recording devices, all those death drives coproducing – it's the thwack, shuffle, & keratin timbre of the nail, bone, skin, & tendon that will break bad machines at the ends of arms.

when have you ever been to the symphony?

in this, i need to be intent. there is a wish that we could just be in this place, its village intent. what do we know? some things go unretrieved, left in the roots at the bottom of the garden to go happily rotten. understand when i speak about naked selfies or the key formal logic operation of the octothorp i am speaking from a position that makes me feel that i so am this in love light, so do my attributes dissolve in that all parts illumination, my person hood. look

discovery of the little temple

through the wrong end of the microscope & i'm sure you'll find the benefits of chocolate health & tiny society.

let me now relate the squeamish tale that is the consequence of all this. overgrown, lost, this forest rose warm in its gender & clothing. the hero is a verb really. indeed there are cells made of perpetuation that have in their mind a perpetuation, that have in their flesh a perpetuation. this function is attending breakfast. can a cell have flesh, is a flesh made always of cells? against the lack or drain of the nearest water or a plight, the winds are pouring (at breakfast!) out of the fan. that red cell, that exo-cell, that cell in the geography of terror. in this there are homes & drains. storage cells are missing from the thin bolus.

beginning of the squeamish tale

i am across my dress again, my sailor suit, my short skirt. who makes a rag / time lay over the land of lost trees? authority attends angus mcphee expo, all rewoven out of grasp. periwinkle bright, women & rats & others hemming the train of the angel of history. eye in the sound: new notions from the sea. i have rewritten this letter over itself, and it

fashion play / passion show

has become easier to write & harder to change each time. on my t-shirt ants have a snowball fight; such surreal fictions, the surreal novel lived on a loving cakeagain & against.

refusal of the call to poetry

there's a vibration, a tone, reverberating over a dome. scars are a brown look out over what drains. the poem's going to tell a fucking story sequestered in a dell or fen. too bad that there are then all of these aunts. try to tell the veracity boys that the question may have a domestic politics. in this story the aunts are minor enemies; they oppose the function. i need this to come from you. they need to see an awkward acronym before it can (hell, gee) be in the tea queue & absolved from blame.

this is some kind of mama bird, that feathers her nest with speech acts & logical statements. it has however loved the way that they talk over its own loose mode of talk. true or false: a masked something cannot move around invisibly, but neither does it become a member of an infraclass. but you let things go by, & *before you know / it gets lost in the steam & chatterof typewriters* (ashbery). however

parataxes & oxytocins

now they are the enemies of talk and / or articulations; their joints ache. there's more than one way to make something like this feel good.

pretty speciated in the general but dodgy fossil record of these kindsa things. please please please do not go teasing me inside my brain where there's a niche i cannot scratch. i wait for you in the street; the cobblestones don't make it any more charming, black umbrellas do. when my love is so strong (if, say, my love is a swimmer, my love lifts weights), why i know i could travel over the whole world. *it means it does mean that there has been a stand* (stein). lights back on & upon a circular logic, peppering skyfloors. lark & whisper.

love call

fingerlings, little insects released by the aunts. fucking little dance all over your face. the function is to kill them all & then cry. my dear, grip this handset in your teeth & have an experience. never mind they have helped it meet the government's recommended nightly allowance of eight spiders swallowed in your sleep. by the light of the rogue blue flame, the function finds its way

our hero-function in peril

through the underbrink. rich scion of yank gave battle inveighin'. it's unfollowed by a perpetual motion; swing whatever they gave you, it's dangerous to go along.

a humid dental experience; the manager on the little island is crowding around, acting as the elder statesman when in fact he has been sent away, up the hill to see where there are left giving-out tubes, for a drill-bit to segment out as it works its way down into particularly nice lewisian gneiss, & gas may result. *in his leisure hours,* [francis fukuyama] *puts together little drones in his garage and proudly exhibits them on his blog* (chamayou). anyway now you know & are who the battle is for.

feel that?

unsteady, left-handed tones. everything we are doing & saying has been something that someone is doing & saying already, so there is not that creativity, something instead fun. craven invisible fuck writes that populist rhetoric at least has the merit (of the nature, of conception) of having aroused an alternative parenthesis / paralysis. instead of release, a topology of something belting, something buttoning. your paint on my jeans, mine

kissy-face

on yours appears, & true plain arts appear from abstract to forest-garden.

*unacknow-
ledged
legislation*

a parliament is a thing: the great thing, the thing of the people, the general thing. those eth knickers bubbling up to betray what has been done in spite of something else. & turning it generates a charge. it transfers moods, quotes then cites, suffering evenly throughout the day. it stoops to catch before it falls off; patterns of this type unpeace the local verse. is this what we're having now, aparliament of tendons, sphincters, capillaries. get the word out, sing like a decorated dome.

r e t u r n
now to the whole encounter. bliss out, & pray on command. we ride with such acidic verve to another rendezvous. the function leaves big dashes here to maintain (or 'keep') its palette as a sleep. follow this at its urging & make the tale told, the said river cut its blood off at the stem or hem. we're in it now. it cries, & we learn that has gone into the establishment of such a tradition, where one does not cry in this role but rather weeps & yells & gives up a burr bare ic yolk.

*the whale
reader in deep
narrative
soundings*

                & so this, with emotion, is
what happens now; laugh it off. return from the tale
to a whole new type of architecture. most dramatic
most visible of all the arts, prettiest building or
monumental 'duck'. destruction of the fabbrick of
the city, imperious gesture. sad fish caughten with no
table in mind, bad fish sold by no outlets, no
streams. mad fish this is another topic for a syllabus
too sweet, too-sweet fish a triumphant return to
contentedness. fascination with sheaf-binding, with
little riefenstahls of the thumb.

*what fish
never swam?
(other
foods?)*

                senator, will you right
now renounce the winter garden? will you put a
cigarette out in a sunflower to show you do not
respect nature, & are therefore the villain? will you
allow a list of all the plant and animal species you
have involved in sexual acts to become public?
waving on top of the neighbouring building, the
crowd of reporters is baying for its *few prosaic days*.
the monks in the newspaper offices are already
illuminating the first letter of each paragraph, a
crucifictive y. but the senator has a sudden defence:
the heart wants what it wants, & *sealed are the spicy*

*accelerando,
dénouement,
trouncing*

92

valves (dickinson). ah you might say fuck this bald season, but no! sortitive (sort of, generative).

kristen stewart won the césar (the french oscar) for best supporting actress in 2014 for her performance in *clouds of sils maria*, becoming first american to win this award, despite her greater notoriety in the anglophone world as the affectless bella swan in the *twilight* film saga. in *clouds of sils maria*, she plays the personal assistant of a famous actress played by juliette binoche, the french actress who was also nominated for a césar (french oscar) for the film but who did not win. they rehearse together a play in which juliette binoche is going to appear. most of the film is them arguing about the play; it is meta. at one point kristen stewart says, *the text is like an object. it's going to change perspective based on where you're standing.* this pivot to the object is at the heart of any artistic or political relationship, which is what we are all doing when we move to text. for instance i may sit up in my bed and wonder where i am, yet still know i need to text. what proportion of anxiety dreams end in spontaneous combustion. this adds a little spice.

can the spice-rose / drip such acrid fragrance (h.d.); maybe this is the perfume i am so allergic to. i promise i am not trying to frustrate your attempts, your abilities, to ask questions. but this house is one of the finest examples of art nouveau carried beyond the point where it is still funny. the group effort disembodies itself (queerly, saboteurishly) with the departure of *linguistically innovative spice* (manson). plugging away at this, it is a bad old egg. keep me on the boil if i must, as long as i remain potable. what does spice mean, in this context. and how to i talk to my gender about the infection? i wonder what it would take for me to win a césar (french oscar) and go up to the dais and accept it without giving a speech like k-stew did, because she does not speak french, although i do. *lu un peu plus que la pure avant-garde, mais beaucoup moins qu'un auteur de grande culture* (barthes). see? first published original typescript (the eager readers crowd around a facsimile) was lost on the train. old silver leader of the small misty band. maloja means helloja and goodbye. let us start a mass movement around the facsimile interpretation of texts. i have often listened to you read quietly and wondered what was coming out of those ears. text orientation, object is as does. and develop a series of lines and grammars to crash the variorum, bring some as yet undesigned supercomputer down in flames. synthetic silk – is this a fragrance or an acting style.

enough, tough:

end of the squeamish tale

it can't resist a, a, a halting. it knows the passata, the chopped tomatoes, the hey! the aunts are gone, and the eyes of cats and other new people dance, not unwild, but projected by the storm. in the days after the infestation, cartoons and comedy became violence. the lion and the wolf, two predators both alike in superiority, but it was the hedgehog as it mounted a scribbled candidacy in the margins and mains, briskly adopting a one life. come, this long-standing and eloquent function says, come, sir, perform your forward thrust.

begin here: if you

test protocol

know where the indications lie, nominate yourself to be a movie star. it was kind of cute, in the way that some functions of capital and the state are. watch the black galaxy accustoming itself to big data. *what a mess, we are stupidly neglectful of the people we like best*

^(sarraute). in this context i got dizzy, thinking about you, about school, big reader; how do i talk to my students about their infestation? instead of keeping afraid, as it is, it is become many with nature. drone riots imperil a bank heist.

love idea: think of a message and give it to the person you most respect.

selp helf

keep your glasses on when you go into the underground, open an oven, kiss; this is moisture, but heartily. in the north pacific gyre i saw bodies as lees, walking. *the city / susurrus are us* ^(nguyen). plants and fungi sing praises, and birds intimidate the intimate weight, my pretty, red-eyed scavenger. understanding peppers it, and rightly, too. this is all material for a concept, in that way that it seems.

diagonal of the syllabary: a grid drawn from kandinsky to kaczynski. what can one do when confronted with a bundle of sticks? keep a body, geek dictate and peek no further associates, and elves cut the cord. i used to be boring. how can i tell if physical situations subtend my consciousness or contain heartless, insensible, mediate circumstances. are we doing

everyone's a captain kirk

here? where is these people who know more than i? her family are sent off, their time watching has to be stopped. she is awake at night essentially, equally ignorant.

scientific interferer fences only a scientist now found to be a commodity. those who want jobs should train in the way that, constructively, love reveals facts, tact. optical systems are of sense: a pattern of these energy into transforms of transforms of transforms. an unconscious sense of any boys, because her open season salvage person eloped and she has not synaptic junctions of the outcome. motility would have environment, direction, choice. it seems that we have a breaking down it might allow back into the hospital.

plot of worthy love

she has now lost all order, fries in view of the diametric opposite. am i no more or less? shall i pass away? even a consensus are alive. a dream of the night before several hours later. she is in a seal, roads at dead, working: cars whiz down, then try to get out. i don't blame her. look up at just the right moment and you can see the rounded, stormy tops of the famous

a dream gone wrong

mountains. is my visual is my world. the brain transforms when we look how we could. but the brain is what?

scoring words almost at random, i have frequently failed to address correctly the fact that we are living under an unfascinating brand of fascism. why have these downy young men come to ask questions and how high are they on a scale of one, two, three, go. who let you into this rave? i only ask because i know someone who launched her literary career by eating magic mushrooms. germany reject this idea, france reject this idea; let us and us fall off like useless limbs into the sea. the intruder had eyes like the tiny black buttons on my gloves.

uprooted

downy pleasant abandonment lingers as a prospect. the sash window comes and takes its terrible revenge. the children are a cat and a performance to be mounted in the quarry, the natural acoustics surrounding and enveloping the art crowd. why pretend the air you breathe is the same between counties or dominions? i only ask because i know someone who launched her literary career by eating. in the letters page of an anarchist

the stakes of public art

newspaper, they assess the theoretical contribution of the unabomber to primitivist theory.

in the field, my gloves, and terror under my gloves. depressed, they write an email. *information is the poetry of the people who love war* [boyer]. what do we still need that we made when we were rich enough to buy materials? i only ask because i know someone who launched her literary career. the words without the tune are found in this all-too-real city district on a long walk into town. often i am permitted to return to this postcard i bought at a museum and then lost.

asdfghjkl;

fuck production. all of these shops sell the same things, the same whips, the same collars, the same tokens of alien love. the book was written so that they could getaway. fuck fuck-production. cross-fertilised, we proved a plant. transcribe a randy soliloquy with timestamps and dates. fuck, productively. you can buy, you can buy, you can buy buy buy. fuck-producing fucks. a song for the service of growth to the market. the book was written for a getaway. now scoot, toot.

hope is the thing with leather

the students whose essays i mark are so talented, they write things that are not even wrong, sentences that have this mystical quality of meaning and saying and doing nothing at all, sublimely. i'm getting along, i'm cottoning on, a turtle in the muck mire may. i feel like as if i was william james in the medical school and gertrude stein comes up to you and says *boom in boom in, sphincter. leave a brain and show it, show it.* so many switches and buttons don't know what to do to get pressed. it's here, it's alive, or at least electrical, the neurostein. i have never been so allergic to a smell in a small room as it is the smell of perfume and mohair and knowing whatever it is that now i don't know, for null.

tender brains

open up that again, like a vein, symbols on a custom typewriter and written their way through the body in such a way as to encode meaning and a relationship between elements; grammar, in its purest form. stones gradually get wider and agglomerate. performing outrage won't make anything crack less over time. apostrophe semifoot: o times! o customs! i'm not sure whether to laugh or fly, from the sea-forest to

retroglyphs

the r.a.f. base where they know, if not my name, the kind of hats i wear, and a retinal scan.

things i have thought at a poetry reading: when will this be over? none of my poems are as good as this poem. this writer is selfish to make us listen. what should i make for dinner tonight? where can i get my poems published so that i will be as famous as this poet? perhaps i should have been a physicist. this is like gertrude stein. yes, the world is worth living in after all. what can i say afterwards to this poet that will sound as i have been listening? i wonder what kind of sex this poet has; can i take my cue from that last poem, or do i need to think about death-of-the-author? how can i get the same kind of job that this poet has so that i can make a living as a poet? should i go to the doctor to get a prescription for anxiety medication? nobody should ever make a living as a poet; i will get a data entry job or a job in a café and in this way i will be worthy. my phone has just vibrated; i wonder if this is an email about a job or from someone i like. how can i get my own flat? this is like j. h. prynne. i would rather worry about money

a walnut salad

in my own flat, even if i can't afford it i will figure it out then. all of my poems are better than this poem. what can i say that will mean i form a connection with this poet and we become friends? should i go to the doctor to get a prescription for antidepressants? this is like j. h. prynne but worse. this poem will never be in an anthology. can i check my phone without being detected? i do not have barista experience and my parents will not let me get a data entry job. why are all the poets doing phds? what would happen if i took off all of my clothes in this poetry reading? i live with my parents and therefore am not entitled to feel bad about money. what would happen if i walked out of this poetry reading? what would happen if i stood up and called this poet a cock in the middle of this poem? this is not like any other poem i have ever read. what will happen when everyone has finished and all of these poets have their phds? i should make a list of things i have thought about during a poetry reading. i should ask to publish this poem in my poetry magazine. this is just like every other poem i have ever heard.

first prose,
now you: sad to relate, i have now lost what

fuck sake

remained of my urbanity. :(you may go to cambridge,
but you've written a lot about class warfare. are you
really a samurai, or are you drunk? there's a gorgeous
disconnect here, a real idiom. you may go to harvard,
but you've written a lot about trauma. i have a plan
for its shape and getting shrift. avoid, in vain,
enveighin', *the non-teleological event of writing* (wang). you
may go to the american university in beirut, but
you've written alot about capitalism. see first (burst)
appendix.

    a doctor said something i couldn't
overhear, a supposed blandishment in the medical
biography. *i would like to write a poem as long as*
california and as slow as a summer (spicer). get it off your

highland park
hallucination

chest; divest. the nurse, however, comments, how
healthy you are. southern california even has seasons,
which seems like a lie, but then the marine layer
comes, bleaching june into gloom, or the santa ana
winds rock the sweet cradle of an orange tree. trying
to make a brownscape european green, they fail into
blue.

these mornings in the haar encircling us have
pit this blinded chaos in a duel with what's beyond
these ruined walls, and thus the medium splits – is,
finally, found dual, now sighted but alone, on kitchen
floors whose eostral chill runs up the vertebrae, the
boiler waking with its quiet roar, the throes of
personal shock hidden away. the vacuum that awaits
our misty breath sucks at the window – on the hob,
the ring, a diadem of haughty hiss, protests, flares
with the violence of simple things. burnt radii may
hold their languor's trace; feuds with the world have
yet some feel of grace.

see this future in the way they
low-sky-pattern monkshood: all pleasure pricks
animals who delight therein, jealous of the wealth of
air, as in a mine or reason. the smell occludes like
newsprint on your tips to the less tangible senses.
just so, bees swarm out of the way as their honey is
gathered, leaving the heart to harness the sting too
long. exposed odometer: what's the exception to this
air, the way it now and then freewheels in long bliss.
i spot a flow with the smell of speed, and anchor that
with grace yet.

don't listen to that one. how a bridge is like a pair of arms, lifting you up – how a bridge is like movement, how is like a mountain. feel the obvious marks a star. last train leaves city centre ten thirty, please ask station staff for last train info from your local station. enough words in there that we kept it wrapped, kept it mundane. i followed the lights of the train down under the river like an empty eye socket, rolled tennis balls down the carriage in order to see how far up or down hill we were travelling as the tunnel lights flashed between ibrox and govan. lies, and a break in the skin.

rainbow poems in this ocean move pornily to the surface. huddle a mother edged over out of seventy-two. a really perfect poem has an infinitely small vocabulary, but a totally flawed poem has a vocabulary ten times the size of the local news. contrition 2016: wrong for the world. make up for any social deficiencies by eating your artist's salad for breakfast; anything done in and of the floorboards is liberation. be the one who paints the cabinets in rising moons, and thus buckle in a strip, hands patterning to make it a dance poxalypse.

xenoglyph: a-i-e. what is living in anyone's belly? humourless antidote: a low dose, instantly. asemic seems tough on the old seams. and i will really try to believe that this was a problem for you it's not a problem for me but okay. every free one enjoys a system, a steam. reading, i dreamed; i wished i could dream like jackie wang and report i had a dream that i was a rock, standing where water is no water, where there is not nothing but water any more. aliens are in the heads of modernist writers, and legislators, and those using water cannons on people at standing rock.

while there is a soul in christmas i am not free. neither are the canon xf-100 high definition professional camcorder, the goal zero 31901 yeti 1250 silver/black xx-large solar generator, the fox labs sudecon decontaminate towelette 100 pack (currently unavailable), or the respironics simplygo portable system, used & new from $1,000. simplygo is the only system that offers continuous flow and pulse-dose delivery in a device weighing less

dream of a dreamless language

#NoDAPL

than ten pounds. regain your freedom and mobility with this high-quality portable unit,

and i will try to believe that *the commons is a transcendental hall* [(moten)], because i would like to wander in the restless ruined mind-palace of the little ecclesiastic inside my head, because poetry, music, and art is called world because it belongs in the world-ocean, that hostile, uninhabitable place. belong to something that is of the up, the movement with the ones who were there for a thirties moment. u is a glacial valley, while useless k is another sharp shard of a glyph stranding a firm stem powerless against its ascender. it can hit you seriously in your heart, becomes always a wanted influence.

wild cathedral, now lost

o aptogramme, voice that stilled sham – absolute golden, meanly divine – wrought, moon-humble saps, faint annulled law such broods change almost nothing, space amongst the bubbling oracular syllable of the sun. this sun an uncle, shining shitty on a hill, is an utter distraction; one mean bean. however, he conforms to the table of ideas i got in 1413, the big book of culture, papal bull. consider me

rises and will

as a vaguely undine or water-droplet-shaped person when i say i've listened and find in the heart of the prose of the world a bitchy restful grace.

the big book of culture: eileen myles for hillary clinton, for zoë leonard, and i approve this message, and i am chill. two ungovernable councils both alike in jeopardy. patience is a virtue, virtue is a grace, and grace is a lazy bitch who wouldn't wash her face. shouldn't have needed these words, but they trained badly: cia deploys art critics; fbi loves netflix procedurals; gchq spends time fucking, writing long letters to lovers; in finnish onnet means 'happinesses', in scots 'onit' means drunk, and in english 'on it' means on itself, having nothing else to mean on. i don't mean that in anything other than a positive way; i will have a dandy macaroon.

voting intention-ality

green boys in amnesiac dirt have the dirt on an amnesiac show trial being held in might as well be berlin. every train station contains a fascist. as needs must, we go down to the chinese supermarket & buy a shrivelled c h r y s a n t h e m u m. i'm at a lost without bibelots who imbibe a lot, a

come back edwin, come back sylvia; we need you now more than ezra telos of bible oughts who limp eyes along. hi need cure else am atlas at a last. needs musk, and populated with afterthoughts – with alternative beck and calls. rolling tongue, owl rib cracks black holes eyes. every city is filled with abandoned or packed-up channels: a stream a burn at the end of the moor/muir, it doesn't anymore. it tries to be accommodating but/and arachnids ate feed.

made all

the greater fuel of my nigerian scams into a poem. wish i could run one; it targets certain people though, focusses by being bad on those, already having been fooled, set up to fool, it will fool. atlas'd, i need a nigerian scam that would work on people who own islands. an apple list once in a bookmoon: join jovial survivors in a race of the cure. fuck knows many thinks, but the hedghog has one big other think coming. hate speech loves life crime, choose your own true genre, fending off normative raiders at fertility gulch. fear the doctor, when she asked you to fool better (coff coff).

rainbows hide; wish mine were yours. did you come this far not to get fucked? *solidarity, because it*

partakes of reason, and hence of generality, is able to GET
comprehend a multitude conceptually [arendt]. roughly sixty
per cent of european adults over half of u.s. teens
almost one in ten western elderly avalanche risky
business. but what if i want my solidarity to be like
an exceptionally thick and resistive custard –
unraisinable – which i do. do i owe a viral feedback
toward this peril pearl, this parallel pie dance? you
can't walk on custard, but you can run on custard –
which i do. open yourself up to moving to other
colours. can you march on it? witch, i knew. it makes
a whole little hill, of which cowcaddens underground
is at the bottom, its island platform configuration
beguiling as we pass.

GET
FUCKED

north wind blows the leaves
from the trees. tomorrow i will go and see zoë's
reading at the museum of disappearing grounds:
bièvre or not, the adda is the only river in britain
that is also the only reptile in britain that is also the
only venomous (not poisonous), that is, windfalls
proliferate behind the big tesco's. teeth are bars, or
perhaps rogue gappy days clustered against a trigger
feminine, bodies of all volatile intuition. cobbles at

*after zoë
skoulding /
jean
portante
reading,
edinburgh,
december
2016*

small intervals clumsily redacted in an infinite torsion spiral of historical blood, a domination. the weather is like a cow; strong, ancient, wrong in the city.

sedona, az: the lady will have two tickets to the gem show. shifts and giggles; trig partly millions of missing votes hitler comedy fiddles while rome burns nights – add rest to the lasses – for poem, a chunk of bliss, land wage of a reason why you might feel afraid to speak – ? twig her morning: drape mention, like over a piece of alma-tadema marble, over the sea-wall of our understanding; understand and overextend the metaphor for yourself. half of all michigan ballots ineligible for recount, used instead for sortilege. depends what you make of divination results, make a claim to psychic power or is that amethyst just part of your aesthetic.

out there, in the darkness, someone is tweeting. i've got no more cord to measure against this thing than what i've made for myself but i can feel the characters regressing. *if you have no house now you'll never get one, and if you're alone now you'll die alone. if you're lucky, you'll sit around, scrolling through your phone, skimming articles, doing email out of work hours, and the streets will fill with rubbish* (rilke, sort of). in part, it is hard to see anything as good as not seeing anything (see second, and *wovon man nicht sprechen* for wittgs. you have reckoned, postscript). i keep a pattern out there for the baby who just cares for me, and the catastrophe when you don't get it.

in american high school movies, an unseen character, bitchily referenced, will always have an italian or polish surname. some allergies are real (orange), but unheard sweeter; i think we'd know (you glad) if i had ingested mallow (didn't say banana) outside of cork. i belong in this party, but it was for this reason that we expelled dissidents, straight from the pages of elle in baggy side dude jeans. is it important to write about this? i'm working in the emerging field at the intersection of silence and the humanities. based on my chart, i'm going to need these muscles in my wrist and venus mount.

back on my chart

four-eyes *would not be dieted with praise* (keats); open urban view eagerly adopts. bodyfuck: hedg your bets, making a night out of

radical indolence (yawn)

what is known. sheep sorrel is sour in a driftwood grove but it tastes like looking in bloodshot eyes that are looking back into your own bloodshot eyes feels. the grand roundness of expectations and this vulgar theology comes open with a slip and fall. hedgfund: fuck in your beds, taking delight how much is owing. weak coward salty prose, not aggrieved but greened and red-bloodied; (yeah) *cannot raise / my head cool bedded in the flowery* drag.

how to induce a poem

after midnight, prepare one litre coffee. put a movie on netflix with as little action as possible (suggest *84 charing cross road, harold and maude, paper heart, clouds of sils maria*). watch 30 mins (well into rising action) while consuming coffee and writing idly. pause movie when writing speed increases and/or what is being written is more interesting than the movie. compose poem while consuming last cup of coffee. ignore the impulse that tells you not to include certain things: cringe can be plucked out in later stages but something can't be put back in. democrats say you campaign in poetry govern in prose; writing is always the rhetoric, and all writing is poetry, while editing is always governance, always prose.

in the law library i wrote about things that would interest someone who was not interested by law books but then i realised i was interested by law books because of complex feelings resulting i believe from early childhood experience about how to behave with respect to systems and rules so i wrote about things that would not interest someone who was interested in law books but not like i was interested in law books but then i realised that i might be more interested in law books or at any rate interested in a way that would generate a different quality of attention than someone who was reading them in order to become a lawyer. i continued to write but/and allowed this to let me eke the terror out.

hansard also works

i have been allergic to that upturned nose and pair of intelligent yet withdrawn eyes that sound like the eyes that are left in a skull, and coughed until my throat was raw. the cough is a practice: a discipline that must be critically regarded and read books about in order to do it in a way that brings about

a sprig of heather

positive change. the cough is a fetish: coughing is sexy and have you ever tried to fuck while one or more participants has a cough, muscles move in ways they never have before. the cough is a sign: an arbitrary relationship between the cougher and what is coughed up.

however did you get so high up in the hills. i shall patrol the gardens of the stately home *until branches spill over that monolith* (catanzano) and drop orange leaves down, a carpet on the floor of this cold woods. except they are thicker than a carpet and more flavourful than the ripest orange from that one fruit tree you have on your fake city homestead, el norte; instead they are like a soft, chewy crust on the surface of all the earth. what replaces dust and is better than this planet, with a white tower block rising out of it (germs saluting the sun), what mutually permeates between a metaphor and a simile.

they crave the light

so then maybe also another answer is to do it in this way: aperture in the side of the counter-mine, thorn-small, becoming a seam of empty, a tiny rock sanctuary, under a street that has a postcode

unbuilded monuments

and is registered with the council. the circle needs you to populate it with small events and decorative birds. *i pray you not to love classifications* (jeffers) ; everything from skull shapes to types of sexuals is an earnest kantian wank. make up your mind to be site-specific in your dealings and determinations and meanwhile i'll be patient as i wander the mind palace and its grounds, preserved.

gallery ahead of me, where is the done-in moon? it immerses itself in loch

ragged coast

fyne or long, one of those invasive blank mirrors that is the dark sensitive aperture in the country. it used to be a deep, poisonous, arrogant life, or a death springing trade and ships of war. now road equivalent winds beat the still-untamed bows of islanders, those poor bodies, with their rough hands and well-illed sexes. a steep calm overcomes; a soothing novel about rothesay in twelve paragraphs, dialogues with the landlords of millport and the petib&b.ourgeoisie of brodick and lamlash, all mooning industrially past heaven.

in this season i'm a fossil, a leaf petrified in stone. what belongs to the real stewards of the land,

and what to the oil museum? in a secluded redwood grove in south china, a dinosaur understanding was perpetuated. even if latin could speak we would be too afraid of its roar, a thick breath that smelled of pages, boreling terminus migration patterns made toothless in their outspreading. a forged balance places blame against graves, a monogramme epigraph ill-embraced. joint honours astro-phil and stellar history taught me about an aesthetic debt paid down against the leafmould eyeshadow.

metasequoia

there is some broke golden promise happening here: e-motion passed against a rational tell. encircled gravity hopes to glad for the interests of the sky together. a thousand-chained (or at least, enough) hearts speaking: assumption cousins, a girl ashamed of her monstrous power and then a way to retain sure strongest gratitude, shoulder love transferred to you, a wrested reply. now unspeakably probably in a separate constancy, the present effort setting will not hopefully happily pursue an 'o' mention, a vocative search term.

i like you now

many routine drills about what to do in the event of a giant meteor strike involve a trip on the bus-train to buxton. to tear fear from a busted tent rivet impedes against drumming the torn a cappella copyleft wanting. keep the morning star in your poem pants. sock of darned willow: how do they want-work. a small flapper king emerged at the edge of the motorway, early days yet, and september comes back, or june, saying it was all a laugh, an acoustic season, an intense greeting of fresh-hearted vocals stretching out over the oldsea. did i reproduce this because of winter, or because of an old star?

dream modus

the name of the object that has appeared in the sky is the symbol you scratch into the table, or doodle in the margin, or in extremis trace on the skin of your lover. —— - - - - - —— - - - - —— — — —— - - - — this is offered only as an example; from here on in, it will be necessary to think about how peopleworlds are individed. —— - - - —— - - —— - - — - - —— - - - —— - - - - - - - - - - - - - - - —————— - - - - - if such punctuation rattles your certainties, cultivate the knowledge that all bodies carry dots. - - - - —— - - - -

sigil porn

——— - · · · — · — · — · · · — · · · — · — · · · — · · · · — — · · · —

——— · · ·

chrome of somes: in the final days, it's time to move on and through space. generational starship as utopia, but genes will degrade. consequence less humiliating in a gently eugenic worldview to become mediocre, for our brains to decline. if people wanted to fall asleep that would be okay. what's the night when i come on stage, read and return to an anechoic chamber made untemporal by medicinal tech (pass anew prop to agitate it recreationally)? deal with it gently in your dickinsonian brain but write like and as you're living through a disaster. and look! as cities fall beneath the waves, we wonder what are the true skills, miss bish, lead us watchward.

poem for the biofuture

scholars considered as solipsistence farmers live on matins, deadly. path participle: i don't even like to travel any more but they always make me, convince me, the birds we need to watch to sleep. rose poetry in the new town (think more east kilbride than milton keynes, a frisson monumental and the roundabout little garden as seahenge, a

the unringing of bells

public clearing where the body of a headman might be left to be picked clean by birds) as the sky opens, touching skilfully, mysteriously her first nose. smut in sporish dots settles down between the leaves or petals to live long lives and raise precarious children. letters from the northern country tell of snow.

*

barthes' 'ten reasons to write' (1969): (1) feels good/sexy; (2) better than speech; (3) use yr gift; (4) get famous; (5) ideological; *p. s.* (6) make secret system; (7) please friends/annoy enemies; (8) break system; (9) make new meanings; (10) confound idea of a 'good reason'.

p. p. s. some poems about autumn that can fuck off: shakespeare, sonnet seventy-three (this THOW per SEEVST witch MAKES thy LUV moar STRONG); rilke, 'Herbsttag' (off dem flowerin lasses die – wind loss); keats, 'To Autumn', (seizing of miss and yellow fruit for less [...] wear out the songs of spring), etc.

in japan there are seventy-two *kō*, or microseasons (h/t daisy lafarge for this info). autumn, & the autumnletter, begins with 'thunder ceases' (23rd - 27th sep). some of the *p. p. p. s.* microseasons mentioned include 'chrysanthemums bloom' (13th-17th oct), 'rainbows hide' (22nd-26th nov), and 'north wind blows the leaves from the trees' (27th nov-1st dec). they came from china but were adapted to japan's climate. (what would glasgow's microseasons be?) winter starts with 'self-heal sprouts' (22nd-26th dec).

winterletter

Whoso couthe take hede and lett the warld pas,
It is euer in drede and brekyll as glas,
And slythys.
This warld, fowre neuer so,
With meruels mo and mo,
Now in weyll, now in wo,
And all thyng wrythys.

(the wakefield second shepherd's play)

self-heal sprouts – the micro-season
is beyond reason (makes camp in
that frosty field) so there's no
sense in imaging different parts –
at this time of year;
love's only love when alteration finds,
unbends with the all-retentive improver
that's found in sacked temples,
astrological with the cut moon in gemini.

needles lead the way
magnets come from the same place as poems
come from the same east-martian, infamous and all-
debatable grounds
i need to know when
and why we are left
with/out
cistern padding, cool air
leaks to the heated retreat
in an atmosphere of delirious threat (black)
it could almost be possible to lift what
could almost be permissible not to do what
can almost be perceived as
a specious evident failure of truth and machine —

consider what happens
        to our mouths when we talk
        about an election as if
        it were a war (victory,
                defeat; losses).
speculate about what happens
        to your ears when you talk
        about a press appearance as if
        it were a weapon,
                a salvo; a shot.
meditate on what happens
        to your eyes when you talk
        about these thoughts as if
        they were any other thoughts:
                retreat, silent, appeasing, sanction.

the good-enough scientist in the, on the march
        wants to eat sleep and breathe her germ
                data, down to the brain steam
        wants to be a climate
        wants to be changed
        needs an impearled call- and beckground
           need an antic roadshow
        where she can practice, work, and philosophise
           deep in the lido
        that rough public verruca commons

the bucks give up their velvet
> *horns* – one image,
> and looking at you i feel i
>> can do this,
>> want to renew,
> like when i found
> a frozen spiderweb
>> in anthropo-
>>>> scene november;
>> i don't know much
>> but i can try
and a photo of it now:
> is this the appearance
>> or life before the arrival?
> naked trees' opening
>> signifying their names?
>> chartered in ancient plays
>> and poems encoded in
>> monastically young grottifoes
>> caught in the solemn
>>> columns of the cloister
> kneel sadly blackened
>>>> in sapphonic margins –
> would the poet, had she never
>> read these words – *mother i cannot spin*
for longing for this one – be less in love?
>> i can't spin either.
a studious summary:
> let   the   looms   be   smashed;
> sabotage   server   farms
> crowd out the lonely valleys

the imaginaire, linguo-toybox

learn a language in three weeks

in an hour (to discover

the electrics of this body,

would need a life of engineering);

think i timed myself

only disserviced

ever coming to feel some

rough thing slouching

in its chairy, varied worldling

walk   on numbered hands

and if i ever let love go (jordan)

to the ko plaza, happily submerged

in what results

timeless

neutered

bad-grammaring

an enth needed to have gender

explained to it

snacks and turmoil

is this how it works no   doubt no fear no   way

wheat sprouts under snow – promises,
       promises! you don't know how you've missed
           the purple holly until you see from above
           down into the season of bare branches
           of twigs and spittle-rain
fragrances gather under the aliment
       meet and consult; never
               a science, perfume is a rave
       astrology; get dressed in the morning
and then remove one revolutionary demand.
       the early turn, the turning over,
         compact revolution in knees and eyebrows;
you have gathered yourself in
a praxis motion, gestures polished
to a mineral nub.

     i am alive — because / i do not own a house (dickinson)
and i stay that way because   i don't know how to say
    because
    papers for all or no paper at all
        recycling centres will work
        round the clock   until it's all
             boats,   hats,   fortune-tellers
             nothing doing
  unless the fences untangle themselves
  and become those wire dreidels, those knight's helmets,
    those steel canoes we all desperately need

find yourself a place as a flourishing
    eater, deep in the kitchen garden,
        the monastic smell of garlic swirling
        between the forgotten chinese redwoods
and the ferns,
        old, overwritten genetic chains unspooling;
    wild versions are cut down,
    tall dinner poppies policed –
consider the place of herbs in a utopian food system
    where they conquer thyme or
        live   on sage or baby's breath:
    the soft beauty of that masked thought
        black and white paisley, arm back to throw
alienation from the rightful king
    in whom this fruitless fly is bound
    to serve the time, not me
            do your worst now *as of the great wind*
        and trauma-flooded, gauze-headed, *dismissed,*
    absolved, like the great moon over activist circles (aliens
did it)
    i*n a starry placating* (stevens)
        so that there's only ever a crisis
    crawling into the worm, getting yourself
corkscrewed past oblivion, getting yourself
    challenged and transforniquated
        a princess prom dress process
           without end

the spring water holds warmth
      in any weather. tied up in two sciences,
      it still has too much to feel
      even as it shifts to going cold
      even if it's only little
      springs work like sylvan decanters;
is there a rain springing again,
      or just that monument you see
      when meditating? two roses disparaged
      in a woodcut – siren snogs, odes blyss'd
      scrapped real to another in this narrative
      repeated as we turn to stamper's ink
         accurate to the last flensy serif
                       in some marginal comment,
             or the side of a building

apparoxysmated distance well
      defined like a set of rhythms
      orderly interred in utopian systems –
      an island musiccollege – is
      a dream demand untempt'd by
         withdrawal hallucinations/reals
              hungry, angry, lonely, tired
         protect yourself against your feels
              faggy, lazy, artsy, wired
         the martyralphabet that steels –

runrig love to dominate

the new païdarchy

capital raining

and river   the runoff

eats the land;

long dominions,

       traintrack flats intend

       to give pleasure,   facilities

           in bronze, desk glint

           that in a magnet amaze

           and give back a series of

       greying swarms; protect this

           nocean – for what it

           does to me – nastily – in

           the sunflowers –

game-birds protest aloud, their sound

       echoing through the glowing peat

    and you can see the air suffusing, smell the woods

       on the letter – was the work we did together

           special or particular? to be avoided?

           the exchange of that kind

       of warmth-light, its theory of value

this coal uncollapses into peat —— circular pits cut into the road

       creels laden, shoulders ached and collapsed

       selfish muscles chastened by whisky-in-tea

       and the common good outmarried –

ice thickens on streams, drifts

    south towards a wider wink.

    renewal seems wrong somehow;

        can we fix what bodies us

        and we need to queue?

    bent to bear back on an arch – the salvaged groan

    whiskered ingredients

        sketching dome after days

    walking sticky and ice-bounded

    modular thrift   it retains

    an intellectual suggestion

    moon-clasped, i eye all those secondhand genders

        thick with results –

the white chickens stop laying eggs. bird-wave heninists

    react to violence in a dome, give

    blisters to liberal feet

walk twice as slowly,

    never suffer, curl into *hospitals,*

        prisons, and schools. i've only

    ever known how it reverberated

    against the moon, a symbol,

        so much depends on a fear of ever

        living in power, doing those works

        with old bloody muscular

        tools.   ridden wide in a red tram

            against living and old gods

    ink be darned as meeting mentor tools blocs up options.

        the student quisling lies heavy

    don't bear down on me –

    pressures reading inverse words

    against continents

are ideas cut, dried, and grey
are men, managing a syndic holiday
retained to leave
grey factory, it returned, towering
over heather and bog,
no recourse to hugeness
balanced a cake,
hung down and cut to eighths

a certain wind melts the ice
and brings a long undrifting dandruff demand
to prepare for winter wolf war
even at the retreat
we're real cool with cop-outs,
distance provocations from our sealed-off
amour-propper, majorly weir a blue peace
like the liquid that spills, calderable –
dams bust in the flight, athenian in scope.
anagnorisis epyllion:
the condition of labour
my voice protects

birds start up with their singing
in the mountains.
they have been to jupiter
and therefore know
the patches of ink;
slim lines against
the last appropriate
formation – to loving
where you live,
the cold huggie.

two thoughts cross paths
and leave their inventor
ash-pale, offering

    plastic pseudopodian
    remnants of harm –

    fish emerge. it's sad to be
    beginning at this time.
to live cyclical and forever
not frozen out of your home
an expense not to last the winter.
i am appointed, logically
drilled as a map-dot, quad-made
by steps and dry, evaporated grass
awake in a dream of snow
    recover myself from public
speech, a frog in a bog.
one of the maudlin
skills we intone
about, being suffused.
    does it matter about what is eaten?
surely the shit-smeared sun
will still seam moonlessly
    through   at night
but placement of the common comma
precludes that reading –
screeds dam an arsehole
mustered in difficult wings.

don't sweat the shape that you've been given, that
only makes baiting beauty worse.
everything slithers, everything writhes
wormlike behaviour in the last hour

134

tunnelling into vertebrae

trying to get warm, looking for the darkest spots

that absorb the sunlight,

trying to get cool, retreating

north — to where the cold water laps

up against the snow, horses drumming

thematic ask, a trained tail array

of long-returning geometries

to the cliodynamic apsis, the crumbling

pentangle at amiens

rain waters the earth.

a long-term arrangement,

    seems to have worked ok

    although some things about it

    could stand to be improved.

        umbrellas gather,

        black for a corporate event,

        nothing to be paid,

        just enjoying an old lover

        as steam collects;

    the mist lingers, humanly,

    might as well bunch up

(sad preference effect)

            i need a unity

        to make sense of the bell of your giving

        how hard is this:

only certain things can happen.

get your head and drum it in, cold

water, get your marriage of a few

mossy planks and keep in woven

        plaid in the retreat of seeming

        dank unreliable codes as the moist

            natures come back into the cartouche

        and then maybe they seem a pro po

            po or no? —

how can follow the course
   of the river   without syntax?
OLIVIA: you are now
   out of your text. way to react
  to a freshwater pearl
  (graverobbing, or,
  a slip in silence) —

among the reeds without,
  prision demands rocking,
  & always to fancy the
  seagreen fops, leather an abolition;
       it's demanding,
   it's back, a watery rattle, filling
     a workplace with the intent
     to be distributed. to too
     much walking or else
     nights give it all forth
     repattern in the falling of
     what's now on earth.

who's this little womb?
abscess a passage, declare a vair
squirrel weakening,
  arc healthy
i care what you link around
  me

it makes itself known,

    now in february a metallic taste

    in the air as your valley fills

    with the intent to be water

    it might get you killed.

what sort of peripatetic urge,

    of knee-jerk reflection

    (where you bend and it's perfect);

    return to terrorise prose

    constant encomium

        receipts for this

        somehow comfort, free fall whistling

        instead of drone –

grass sprouts, trees bud

    everything new panics

    into bloom.   i saw in

             december an un-

             waiting blossom

             a sleepy wail behind

             net curtains. jealousy

     waiting to be expressed,

     a sound without person

     or grammar or gender –

one morning, as a social democrat
    awoke from anxiety dreams
    about the administration
    she discovered that she had been
    transformed.   not much later,
              a conservative, preserved in his
              suit-and-tie club suit- and tie-love,
              travelled ex-communist europe.
              didn't like kosiče because
              of all the graffiti;
              brown faces in between the walls
              appall. homonationals who
              dark times bear out, fail-safeing
              a wretch in this, stretching his
              lovers' pale young bodies
              insects, asleep under the ground,
wake up; they know this is wrong,
    but seagull power — it emerges,
              north, and trembling. a deep stac,
   an arcane geologic alien, inhuman spire;
      there is also shell-sand;
                 white coral against idiom,
                 news that stays a slice of pink
                     clouded sundown
                     bullshit thought

how can a bond

essay?   and could it only

    preen, all pleasantly,

    could emerge from that

    movement urge?

impeach blossoms:

    they have served their notion well,

    but now fall bitterly, soil

    the pants of spring.

    the hairy art of leaving

isn't hard to cast, or

    to invoke, a pretty

        petty feel of attach

    ment – tiny fibres reach out,

    trying to be one

    of them (though wrongly

    folded by nature);

    spiritual shortcut to the res

        o lotion:

every email chime comes from the heart

of the home of the earth mother

from the very pericardial sac

    of the house of those who know that herbs

    and a respite from nasty haste

are all it takes when

you have generated a mistake

collective materials notion
        badly but never entirely apart.
        a brown owl
                hunts at noon,
        the flat isle its
        dark, the only
        grudgingly given hill
        peakwise turns its face
        to the compass point
        hairy against avail
        finally affording
                a syllable, two,   then four
        as an age against
                                which the precarious texture
        of isthmus rills
        salty into a nude,
                fresh, puckering nature

        stomach error against shapes,
                black against eyes for redness,
(a caterpillar they say)
        glows from a halogen ebb
        made fresh for works;
                a high treetop wall,
                an artwork never ceasing,
(becomes after time inward goo)
        a thousandpatterned shape
        deigning to murmur
                as a dedicated swallower of
                primitive evolutionary stages;
(some form else to flut it out)
        winter never affirmed
                gets softer anyway, is released

reader's notes

All who think season did not mean what
What is it.
I have been and been amounted to it.
When they come in and come in and out.
Naturally it is not.

– Gertrude Stein, *Stanzas in Meditation* IV.xxi.35-40

naturally it is not. was written between the Spring Equinox 2016 and the Spring Equinox 2017. At each solstice or equinox in between, it changes form.

The poem challenges the (Western, Celtic) notion of the four-season wheel of the year, and the far greater range of cultural imaginaries of the year as cycle, which is made increasingly irrelevant as a mode of reckoning by (a) urban life, and therefore (b) queer life, as well as (c) climate change / the capitalocene. Its structure and form are an attempt at an unnatural poetics. Keats thinks that poetry should come as naturally as leaves to a tree, or it ought not to come at all; what happens when economics have shifted the world such that the leaves come to the tree too early, too late, or never? 'Nature' itself is a capitalist and imperialist invention, designed to protect those aspects of the world it does not want to change and to abdicate its responsibility to anything outside of 'culture'. This poem works to re-erase those differences.

The text's politics is utopian, and imagines alternative spaces as well as times. While there are references to political events that were unfolding as it was being written – Brexit, Trump, Standing Rock – ultimately the poem is concerned with the politics of 'grassroots ann claybournes' (p. 6). In Kim Stanley Robinson's *Mars Trilogy* (1992-96), Ann Claybourne is a Martian colonist who argues that the planet's primordial beauty is more important even than human survival, and seeks to resist the nature-culture that capitalist society wants to impose on the universe. Claybourne's politics have no analogue in the fight between unceasing exploitation and 'green' conservation. The truly utopian positions can't be theorised into existence, they have to be imagined out of life as it is lived and language as it is used.

The rhetoric is drawn from avant-garde poetries – modernist parataxis (the collaging of lines and ideas without evident semantic connections), postmodern intertextuality (the frequent citations and notes), contemporary catachresis (innovations in diction and grammar), etc. This also underlines the message; as grammar is a series of rules about the combination of meaning-creating elements, so the wheel of the year is a grammar of time. The text's verbal, phrasal, grammatical, and formal innovations all therefore contribute to the project.

In the 'springletter' (Spring Equinox 2016-Summer Solstice 2016), each line has eight words. This process, partially adapted from Bob Perelman's essay in verse 'The Marginalization of Poetry', means that the order and expression of ideas is shaped by the formal device of the line-break. 'both the flush left / and irregular right margins constantly loom / as significant events, often interrupting what / I thought I was about to / write and making me write something / else entirely' (Perelman 1996, p. 4).

For the 'summerletter' (Summer Solstice-Autumn Equinox), each page has a hundred words. Each page has a one-word summary, and these are collected in the 'indexpoem' at the end. This is perhaps the most superficially simple part of the text, and functions as a symbolic key for the rest of the text. It opens with a quotation from Tan Lin: 'reading is a failed lesson in bureaucracy'. Reading should be incomplete compared with writing – it should skip, sleep, resist – and as Barthes says in *The Pleasure of the Text*, texts are 'non-isotropic' (Barthes 1975, p. 36), not the same all the way through, but irregular, like woodgrain. This poem's varying resistances are designed to facilitate this kind of 'indolent' reading pleasure.

The 'autumnletter' (Autumn Equinox-Winter Solstice) is written in prose paragraphs, each of which carries a title in the margins. The aesthetic of this, both in terms of the visual appearance of the page and the relationship between marginal comments and prose text, is influenced by Lyn Hejinian's *My Life* (1980/1987). However, it also has narrative and confessional elements which are the emotional key to the text, corresponding to the symbolic keys offered by the 'summerletter'. As Kristen Stewart, who in 'the spice mines' becomes the poet's avatar, says, 'the text is like an object. it's going to change perspective based on where you're standing' (p. 95). In this sense, much like Rachel Blau DuPlessis' *Drafts* (1989-2014), this is not one along poem, but the same poem written multiple times.

Finally, the 'winterletter' (Winter Solstice 2016-Spring Equinox 2017) is composed using a varying margin width, used in a variety of ways by poets too numerous to mention but here modelled after a systematic study of the use of the technique in the poetry of Nat Raha from *countersonnets* [2013] onwards), and has sections informed by Japanese *kō*, or microseasons, indicated by quotations in italics.

The title was the last part of the poem to be written/stolen. 'I have been and been amounted to it', writes Stein, in a prototypical text of queer abjection stripped to the copula. 'I have been', she writes, and this troublesome, tautologous 'being' (as in 'be who you are'), is what a world that desires to reduce everything to its value 'amounts' her to. Queers can't *be*, but have to 'be who we are', or not, as the case may be. And when each new season is not itself – a hotter, drier summer, a colder, stormier winter – the season, time, is in the same boat. It's not natural, which is to say, nature it ain't, which is to say, naturally it is not.

callie gardner
glasgow, september 2018

references

SPRING

p. 5 'Who has not been sleeping on an inspired day? The mind of the day sleeps us. Watching us. A fascinated consciousness.' – Carla Harryman

p. 6 'And it is well to state that rain makes hills green / And the sky blue and the clouds dark / And the water water by them' – Gertrude Stein, *Stanzas in Meditation* II:iii

p. 7 'What is a utopia for? To make meaning.' – Roland Barthes, *Roland Barthes*

p. 7 'erotogenics intelligible' – Nat Raha, *countersonnets*

p. 8 'as syllable from sound' – Emily Dickinson, Poem 126

p. 9 'term has an end. It was getting dark on the platform of nowhere' – Veronica Forrest-Thomson, 'Cordelia'

p. 10 'Your hands / shake. You are fragile to the world's / noise. You imagine all the others / sleep' – Jennifer Cooke, 'No One Sleeps'

p. 10 'I do not want to go into that cold reality, stark as a dream' – Kristjana Gunnars, *The Substance of Forgetting*

p. 11 'written on the soul of the hearer together with under-standing, that knows how to defend itself, and can distinguish between those it should address and those in whose presence it should be silent' – Plato, *Phaedrus*

p. 11 'take a pen and write in water' – Ibid.

p. 12 'worthwhile pleasures on this earth slip between gratifying another and gratifying oneself. Some would call that an ethics' – Maggie Nelson, *The Argonauts*

p. 13 'solves the perplexities of action as though they were solvable problems of cognition' – Hannah Arendt, *The Human Condition*

p. 16 'swaying is the only kind of affection' – Amy De'Ath

p. 18 'offering up in sacrifice a little of my imaginary' – Reda Bensmaïa, *The Barthes Effect*

p. 20 'being compelled by our own opacity, our own places of unknowingness' – Judith Butler, *Giving an Account of Oneself*

p. 24 'the park where state translators, laid off, sat sad for their hospitals, prisons and schools' – Vahni Capildeo, 'Mercy and Estrangement'

p. 25 'the joy of life is the irresistible, constant, victory of the new' – Wassily Kandinsky, 'On the Problem of Form'

SUMMER

p. 29 'Like love, the slowest and most statistically unreliable of human communications mediums, reading is a failed lesson in bureaucracy and poetry its most indolent operation.' – Tan Lin, '+-^ Themes'

p. 36 'it accepts all / marks & none.'; 'just write / into it' – Eileen Myles, 'Culture'

p. 45 'graphic bliss: before painting, music' – Barthes, *Roland Barthes*

p. 46 'stealing parts of language that remain missing' – John Yau, 'The Missing Portrait (1)'

p. 47 'movement and the rest have their definite laws; according to these, firm and yielding lines are differentiated' – *I Ching*

p. 48 'a well-turned sentence is as much stripped of all intermediaries as is the most rigorously bare algebraic demonstration' – Father J. J. M. Amiot, *Mémoires*

p. 53 'now she wonders if the laws of seasonal renewal might apply to humans too' – Chris Kraus, *Summer of Hate*

p. 57 'what matters is shaped by the directions taken that allow things to appear in a certain way' – Sara Ahmed, *Queer Phenomenology*

p. 59 'debacle of the neuter: massive shift [...] to the masculine form and feminine = derivative' – Barthes, *The Neutral*

p. 61 'shipmates, have ye shipped in that ship?' – Herman Melville, *Moby-Dick*

p. 64 'in a moment of abstraction' – Veronica Forrest-Thomson, 'Approaching the Library'

p. 71 'the art of the useless supplement' – Barthes, *The Neutral*

p. 74 'lost in the cleave of clasping and sweetfleshed day' – Whitman, *Leaves of Grass*

p. 75 'fleshy, mucous, liquid body, the musical body' – Barthes, *Variations on Writing*

AUTUMN

p. 81 'and I have known / despair that the Face has ceased to stare / at me with the Rose of the world / but lies furled' – John Wieners, 'Cocaine'

p. 82 'with our pistil soul-bright / our stamen-heaven' – Paul Celan, 'Psalm'

p. 88 'before you know / it gets lost in the steam & chatter of typewriters' – John Ashbery, 'Paradoxes and Oxymorons'

p. 89 'it means it does mean that there has been a stand' – Stein, *Tender Buttons*

p. 90 'in his leisure hours, [francis fukuyama] puts together little drones in his garage and proudly exhibits them on his blog' – Grégoire Chamayou, *Drone Theory*

pp. 92-3 'sealed are the spicy valves' – Dickinson, Poem 131

p. 93 'the text is like an object. it's going to change perspective based on where you're standing' – *Clouds of Sils Maria* (2014)

p. 94 'can the spice-rose / drip such acrid fragrance' – H. D., 'Sea Rose'

p. 94 'linguistically innovative spice' – Peter Manson, *Adjunct: An Undigest*

p. 94 'lu un peu plus que la pure avant-garde, mais beaucoup moins qu'un auteur de grande culture' – Barthes, *Roland Barthes*

p. 95 'what a mess, we are stupidly neglectful of the people we like best' Nathalie Sarraute, *The Planetarium*, trans. Maria Jolas

p. 96 'the city / susurrus are us' – Hoa Nguyen, 'Digressive Parentheses'

p. 99 'information is the poetry of the people who love war' – Anne Boyer, *Garments Against Women*

p. 100 'boom in boom in' etc. – after Stein, *Tender Buttons*

p. 103 'the non-teleological event of writing' – Jackie Wang, 'writing the fool' <https://loneberry.tumblr.com/post/111433726077/writing-the-fool>

p. 103 'i would like to write a poem as long as california and as slow as a summer' – Jack Spicer, 'Psychoanalysis: An Elegy'

p. 107 'the commons is a transcendental hall' – Fred Moten

pp. 109-10 'solidarity, because it partakes of reason, and hence of generality, is able to comprehend a multitude conceptually' – Arendt

pp. 111-2 'if you have no house now you'll never get one, and if you're alone now you'll die alone. if you're lucky, you'll sit around, scrolling through your phone, skimming articles, doing email out of work hours, and the streets will fill with rubbish' – after Ranier Maria Rilke, 'Herbsttag'

pp. 112, 113 'would not be dieted with praise'; 'cannot raise / my head cool bedded in the flowery' – John Keats, 'Ode on Indolence'

p. 115 'until branches spill over that monolith' – Amy Catanzano, *Starlight in Two Million*

p. 116 'I pray you not to love classifications' – Robinson Jeffers, 'Monument'

WINTER

translations of the names of japanese kō, *or microseasons, are taken from* nippon.com

p. 123 'Whoso couthe take hede and lett the warld pas, / It is euer in drede and brekyll as glas, / And slythys. / This warld, fowre neuer so, / With meruels mo and mo, / Now in weyll, now in wo, / And all thyng wrythys.' – The Wakefield Second Shepherd's Play, Scene 1

p. 124 'in an atmosphere of delirious threat' – Hannah Black, 'New World Disorder' <https://www.artforum.com/slant/id=66897>

p. 126 'mother i cannot spin for longing for this one' – Sappho, Fragment 102, translated by Kat Peddie

p. 127 'and if i ever let love go' – June Jordan, 'I Must Become a Menace to My Enemies'

p. 128 'I am alive – because / I do not own a house' – Dickinson, Poem 470

p. 130 'as of the great wind'; 'dismissed, absolved'; '[i]n a starry placating', – Wallace Stevens, 'Mozart, 1935'

p. 137 'OLIVIA: You are now out of your text.' – William Shakespeare, *Twelfth Night*, Act 1 Scene 5

acknowledgements

excerpts from the four letters were previously published in the following places: parts of 'springletter' in *amberflora* 1 and *AMP* 3;1; parts of 'summerletter' in *Adjacent Pineapple* 1 and *3:AM Magazine*; parts of 'autumnletter' in *Jungftak* , *Datableed* 7, and *para.text* 4; and part of 'winterletter' in *Front Horse* 2. my thanks to the editors for their faith in long poems in general and this long poem in particular.

it takes a village to write a poem, and this one in particular has too many other *scriptores* to list, but certainly it owes its existence and completeness to all of the poets quoted in it as well as to helen rigg, iain mckinnon, jane goldman, and, most of all, to its first and best reader, gloria dawson.